MERRIMAN'S HAWAI'I

MERRIMAN'S
HAWAI'I

PETER MERRIMAN
and Melanie P. Merriman

PHOTOGRAPHY BY LINNY MORRIS

story farm

WINTER PARK · SANTA BARBARA · BERKELEY · HONOLULU

Merriman's Hawai'i
Copyright © 2022 by Peter Merriman

All rights reserved.
No portion of this book may be copied or distributed
without the express written permission
of the author and Story Farm, LLC.

Published in the United States by Story Farm, LLC.
www.story-farm.com

Library of Congress Cataloging-in-Publication data
is available upon request.

ISBN: 978-0-9905205-8-0
PRINTED IN CHINA

ART DIRECTION: Albert Chiang
EDITORIAL DIRECTOR: Veronica Randall
PROOFREADING: Dorothea Hunter Sönne
RECIPE DEVELOPMENT AND TESTING:
Melanie P. Merriman and Barbara Pratt
INDEXING: Amy Hall
PRODUCTION MANAGEMENT: Tina Dahl
PERSONAL ASSISTANT TO CHEF MERRIMAN: Lizzie Harris

10 9 8 7 6 5 4 3

THIRD EDITION 2022

This page and facing page: Waimea. Around 1942, the US Postal Service
changed the name of this Big Island upcountry community to Kamuela.
Most folks living here prefer its original Hawaiian name, Waimea.

Food alone is no fun at all.
This book is dedicated to my wife, Victorine,
who makes all meals better,
and with whom I've been honored
to have shared the entire journey.
It would have been no fun without you Vic!

Foreword

BY RICK BAYLESS

THE FIRST TIME I met Peter Merriman was in 1993 during my first trip to Hawai'i, a place I'd never had on my radar. To my then un-schooled mind, Hawai'i was just one big Cancun, and I'd never much enjoyed going to Cancun. But I'd been invited to an important chefs' summit on the Big Island, so I packed my bags. I should have packed tremendous expectations, too, because I landed in Kona's tiny airport and stepped into a magical land that, to this day, holds a place of exotic won-der in my memory.

Perhaps I said hello to Peter during the conference—I know he was the muse be-hind so many of the thrilling experiences and tastes I encountered over the few days I was there—but I honestly don't recall. I was too infatuated with the fishing expe-ditions, the cooking demos and the luau hosted by the taro farmers in Waipio Valley.

No, it wasn't until I drove from the Kona coast, where our summit had taken place, up the road to Waimea to Merriman's res-taurant that I felt I really met Peter. I really met him as I tasted plates of stun-ning local opah and ono gilded with the freshness of island herbs and tomatoes and greens—ingredients that all the hotel chefs had said had to be brought from the mainland. I basked in Peter's effervescent enthusiasm for the beef and lamb from a nearby farm and the engagingly ripe fruit that had been delivered by an old hippy homesteader he'd met somewhere along the way.

Long before anyone had coined the phrase "farm-to-table," Peter saw the true possibilities in Hawai'i's land and in the people that sur-

rounded him. All these years later, those nascent possibilities have blossomed into everyday pleasure for so many, and Merriman's in Waimea has begotten seven more opportunities for folks to enjoy delicious food that celebrates the bounty of Hawai'i's islands and those who so beautifully craft that food.

As I leaf through the inspiring pages of *Merriman's Hawai'i*, my only regret is that the all this vivid deliciousness remains a half-day plane ride from Chicago, where my home fires burn.

Island Style

I STARTED COOKING because I was hungry. In fact, I'm still hungry—all the time.

I grew up in McKeesport, a mill town suburb of Pittsburgh. My father, like most of the fathers, worked for US Steel, and like most kids in the neighborhood, I played football and worshipped the Steelers. Unlike most of the other kids, I was passionate about food and cooking. Remember that lima bean they gave us in first grade to bring home and germinate? My mother swears I planted mine in the backyard and immediately started planning how I would cook and eat the beans when they grew.

My mother, Woody Merriman, was a journalist at the *McKeesport Daily News*. In the 1960s, under her nom de plume of Mary McKee, she covered the household beat, what we used to call home economics. Her column included recipes for the home cook, and every one of them had to be tested. It didn't take long for my smart mother to figure out that she could get her recipes tested, and satisfy my enormous appetite by exploiting my interest in cooking.

When I was 14, I made eggs benedict on an open fire and won the Boy Scout Camporee cooking contest. Man, I was on my way! A couple of years later, I invited my football team to dinner, and I'm pretty sure that was the first time any of those guys had salade niçoise with fresh steamed artichokes.

That same year, I got a lucky break. Ferdinand Metz was the head chef at HJ Heinz based in Pittsburgh. Metz was one of America's greatest chefs. In the 1970s, he taught a gourmet cooking class in the evenings, and I landed the job as his unpaid kitchen helper. He opened my eyes to what great cooking can be. He taught his students to make oxtail soup—who knew you could make something so good with a cow's tail? As the Heinz company chef, he had access to truckloads and train cars full of ingredients. He taught me that selecting the very best of these ingredients was the first step to a memorable meal. To this day, I still use variations on some of his recipes, and I

When I was 14, I made eggs benedict over an open fire and won the Boy Scout camporee cooking contest.

always focus on the integrity of ingredients.

At the end of high school, I was accepted at the Culinary Institute of America (CIA), and I also got an offer to go to the University of Pennsylvania as a member of the football team. I struggled with the decision right up until the day I visited Penn. As soon as I walked into that gorgeous 75-year-old stadium, Franklin Field, and saw those 53,000 stadium seats, I said, "I'm coming here."

At Penn, I only played football for two years, but I never lost my hunger or my passion for cooking. I lived in a big house off campus with 14 other guys. Every Saturday night was "dinner club." I cooked for all the guys in the house and anyone else who showed up. On Saturday mornings, I rounded up two or three housemates, and we borrowed a car or took the subway to the Italian market in South Philly. We made several passes along the main block of the market, stooping under the colorful metal awnings to sample sausages, or sliced fruits. Remembering what I'd learned from Chef Metz, I went in close to smell the fresh fish (which should be almost odorless) and examine the beef to make sure it was uniformly red and well marbled. I squeezed tomatoes and shook the heads of lettuce, slowly composing the night's menu in my mind. We always stopped at Isgro Pastries for their incomparable cannoli. They were truly handmade, and the best I've ever eaten.

After graduation in 1978, I was offered two amazing opportunities—a job as a res-taurant manager at the World Trade Center in New York City, and a chef's apprenticeship program with RockResorts. The New York job started immediately and the apprenticeship didn't start until late fall, so I accepted both. By September, I was certain. I wanted to cook. Off I went to the Woodstock Inn in Vermont to start working under Chef Hans Schadler.

The RockResorts apprenticeship transitioned me from a home cook to a professional. Anyone can make a niçoise salad, even for 20 football players, but professional cooking is about consistent production. I had to learn how to make multiple dishes for multiple diners, night after night. I gained a whole new set of skills, including how to cook in an organized yet rapid manner, how to set up my mise en place, and how to plan ahead for the next hour, and the next day. I cooked at every station—pastry shop, hotline, garde manger, roasting, grilling and sauces. I learned about sanitation and how to clean and stock the walk-in. There was one thing though that I could not learn at the Woodstock Inn—butchering. I was transferred to the Grand Teton Lodge Company in Jackson Hole, Wyoming, for one summer. I loved butchering, and it gave me a real appreciation for using every part of any animal. Living in a national park and getting out into the mountains was the best part of that summer. I camped out most nights on the banks of the Snake River, catching and cooking cutthroat trout over an open fire, then hightailing it back to the butcher shop by 7 a.m. each morning.

I learned so much from Chef Schadler, more than I can express. Perhaps most importantly he instilled in me the professionalism and discipline that great kitchens require. He showed me that chefs could live in the most beautiful places in the world, but our devotion was always to the craft. Play hard and work harder—this was the lesson that I would carry with me always.

After my apprenticeship, I spent a year as commis de cuisine at the Intercontinental Hotel in Frankfurt, Germany. Do not be fooled. Commis de cuisine is just a way of saying low man on the kitchen totem pole. From top to bottom, you have the chef de cuisine, the sous chef, the chef de partie and, finally, commis de cuisine. At least

From left to right: **Chuck Maser, Peter Merriman, Fran Gavin and Jimmy Kaden on graduation day.**

I had gone up one rung to being a journeyman, no longer an apprentice. The German kitchen taught me a lot, most importantly attention to detail. Everything on the plate matters and must be the very best possible.

By 1982, I found myself cooking at the Four Seasons in Washington, DC, but the job wasn't to my liking. I quit on a gray, wintery day and headed home to my brother-in-law and sister's apartment where I'd been bunking. My brother-in-law, Paul, grew up in tough South Boston and is a no nonsense kind of guy. He greeted me with, "You got to start looking for a job—no room for unemployed bums around here."

Before I could even think up a snappy response, the phone rang. It was Chef Hans-Peter Hager offering me a job at the new Mauna Lani Bay Hotel on the Big Island of Hawai'i. I barely knew where Hawai'i was, but I knew it was warm and exotic. I missed the feeling of being someplace distinctive that I'd had in Europe, and I wanted a new adventure. I said, "When can I start?" He said, "Monday." Paul's reaction was unforgettable. "Are you kidding me? You're the only #$@&%*! in the world who is unemployed for just 15 minutes—and you land a job in Hawai'i!"

This was long before the Internet, so I headed to the library to learn what I could about Hawai'i. I knew it was a state, and that it wasn't like any state I'd ever visited. Who lived there? Did they speak English? What was the cuisine like? I learned the Hawaiian islands are basically in the middle of the Pacific Ocean. The people living there came from all over Polynesia, and all over the world—Japan, China, Korea, Portugal and the Philippines. I was salivating as I imaged the cuisine that would reflect all these cultures.

While the only agricultural products mentioned were pineapples and sugar, the encyclopedia descriptions of rain forests, and drier areas suggested they must have been growing all kinds of produce. Plus there were pictures of coconuts, mangos, and several tropical fruits unfamiliar to me. Next I read about the fish—huge fresh tuna, and

so many species I'd never heard of, like ono, opakapaka, and mahi-mahi. I couldn't wait to get cooking.

I left DC thinking I'd stay in Hawai'i a year; then I landed in Honolulu. As I walked along the open-air concourse toward the inter-island terminal to catch my flight to the Big Island, I peeled off my jacket, felt the warm breeze, and smelled the perfume of plumeria blossoms. It had been a long flight and I actually thought I might be dreaming. Whatever it was, I wanted more.

After a 40-minute flight, I was in Kona, where T. Lowe, one of the other cooks picked me up drove me through the lava fields to my new home. I was surprised to learn that I would be staying with other cooks from the competing hotel, the Mauna Kea. (Read more about this in A Room with a View on page 186.) I soon realized that sharing is a local tradition—if you have something, and someone else needs it, you let him or her use it. This kind of respectful cooperation is one of the things I love about Hawai'i.

Within days, I was cooking on the line and stunned to find that the cuisine was the same continental style I'd been cooking on the East

I left DC thinking I'd stay in Hawai'i for a year, maybe two—then I landed in Honolulu. . . . I peeled my jacket off, felt the warm breeze and smelled the perfume of the plumeria blossoms. It had been a long flight, and I actually thought I might be dreaming.

Coast—steak béarnaise, veal Marsala, poached lobster, and sole almondine using frozen fish! I had to leave the hotel where I cooked for a living to find food worth living for.

The athlete in me was loving the active life in Hawai'i. My line cook job started around 2 p.m. each day and I worked until 10. Mornings were for biking, hiking, diving and trying to surf. Within a month of my arrival, I joined the Kawaihae Canoe Club. Just after dawn every morning, I'd get into an outrigger with Hawaiian, Filipino, and Japanese locals and paddle in the shadow of Mauna Kea, the giant, often snow-capped, volcano. Saturdays were race days, and afterwards we headed to the beach to enjoy a potluck. This food, served out of plastic containers and foil pans, really got my juices flowing—and everything, except the Spam, was local. Japanese members brought homemade sushi; Chinese paddlers made beef broccoli; Filipinos served pork adobo; the Koreans brought kimchi; and the Hawaiian guys brought squid luau, poi and little steamed packages of taro leaf stuffed with meat called lau lau. I started dreaming about how I would bring these flavors to a restaurant setting, but first I had to learn how to cook like a local. (See Chapter 7, Cooking Like a Local, for some of my favorite recipes from the potlucks.)

Right about that time, my boss at the Mauna Lani put me in charge of the employee cafeteria. The employee menu reflected the cultures of the people who worked at the hotel:

Monday was kalua pork and cabbage; Tuesday was chicken long rice; Wednesday was shoyu chicken; and kimchi and Spam musubi were served every day. I think the cafeteria cooks saw me as a cocksure kid from the mainland, more football player than chef. I could see they knew what they were doing and, for the most part, I stayed out of their way. But I was watching, occasionally asking a question, trying to absorb the local knowledge.

When they saw how sincere I was, the cafeteria cooks took me under their wing. These generous 'ohana—Big Al and Willie Pacatang, Aunty Bertha and others—not only showed me how to make flavorful dishes, they also taught me that local food was about much more than ingredients and recipes. My teachers poured their gratitude for life in Hawai'i, and the riches it offers, into every dish. They shared their expertise while expecting nothing in return, and they genuinely rooted for my success. Now, when I make my version of chicken shoyu, cucumber namasu or any of a hundred dishes, every bite is infused with my love and appreciation for the people of the islands.

Two years into my Hawai'i adventure, I was hooked. I had become attached to the magnificent landscape; rich culture and ethnic traditions; unique history (including the abdication of the last Hawaiian Queen less than 100 years prior to my arrival); and speaking pidgin—like, *That shrimp luau broke da mouth* (tasted really good), or *I was ono for some pork adobo* (ono is a fish, but also means to have a craving). I loved the people—so humble, down-to-earth, connected to nature, and full of respect for the land and for each other. I wanted to stay long enough to become kama'aina (literally, child of the land, or someone who was born or has lived in Hawai'i for a long time). Still, after less than two years of cooking the same things on the line every day, I needed a new challenge. So I applied for the position as head chef of a new restaurant opening soon on the grounds of the Mauna Lani Resort.

The Gallery restaurant would feature steak and lobster—not inspiring, but at least I would be the boss and learn something about the business. I had started to dream about owning my own place one day, and I knew I would need to learn more about the management side

of a restaurant. At only 28 years old, with no experience as a head chef, I figured I was a long shot to get the job, but I was also young enough and brash enough to try. At the end of a fairly straightforward interview, the newly appointed general manager asked me, "If you could do any kind of cuisine in this new restaurant, what would you do?"

I figured it was a rhetorical question, since The Gallery was already slated as a steak and lobster place. "I'd do regional cuisine," I said.

"Like what?"

"I'd serve locally caught fish and locally raised meat, with locally grown vegetables and fruits, cooked in ways that reflect the local culture. I'm surprised that none of the restaurants here feature foods unique to Hawai'i."

I wasn't surprised that my answer ended the interview. But I was shocked when the GM called a few days later to say I was hired.

"You got the job, and we also want to do that regional cuisine thing you talked about," he said.

I thanked him, hung up the phone, and smacked myself in the forehead. It was a perfect example of "be careful what you wish for." I had casually tossed out the idea of regional cuisine—and now I had to figure out how to do it! The truth is, regional cuisines are not invented, but discovered. We set about taking family cooking traditions and tweaking them for restaurant use. Simultaneously, we pursued the bounty of crops, seafood, and livestock available locally.

Opening The Gallery felt like a Silicon Valley start-up. It would be different from any other Hawai'i restaurant. I hired a young, talented

Peter Merriman *(top row, far left)* and fellow paddlers at the conclusion of a regatta, Hilo.

and adventurous culinary team. Sandy Barr, who worked with me at the Mauna Lani came along, and later became chef at Merriman's. Brad Hirata, a surfer from Hilo, and Bobby Nakamura, who also grew up in Hawai'i answered our newspaper ads and, man, could those guys cook! Calvin Escorpeso came on

It was a perfect example of "be careful what you wish for."
I had casually tossed out the idea of regional cuisine—and now
I had to figure out how to do it!

board as dishwasher (we worked together at three different places, over 20 years) and brought with him his mother's recipe for cream pie. (Check out the recipe for Strawberry Cream Pie in Chapter 8.) I planned to introduce a prix fixe menu with several courses and I was determined to harvest the land and the sea right outside the door for every course.

Some of the sourcing was just a matter of driving around and talking with folks. I found a local butcher selling island-raised beef. I hung out at the docks and chatted with the fishermen about what kind of fish I could get on a regular basis. On one of my many trips to the SureSave grocery, the butcher told me they bought Hawai'i-raised chickens from O'ahu, and I convinced him to order two extra cases every week for the restaurant.

Some of the sourcing was pure luck—like the time I was in the Waipio Valley for a photo shoot on taro. I started up a conversation with the taro farmer and found out he also raised edible snails. So I created a snail dish for The Gallery. Or the time I was on the tarmac waiting to board an inter-island flight at the Waimea airport and saw a crate of pheasants. I quickly jotted down the information about the pheasant farm printed on the box, and gave them a call when I got back to the Big Island.

Much of the sourcing involved personal initiative. One day I was trying out a curry recipe and ran short of coconut. Believe it or not, fresh coconut was hard to come by back then.

On a whim, I walked outside and climbed a tree to retrieve one. One of the guys from the maintenance crew saw me, and promised to bring me the coconuts whenever they trimmed the palm trees on the property. The maintenance guys also made me a special kind of hook so I could harvest sea urchins off the rocks in the shallow waters near the hotel, and for a while I was known as the chef who climbs trees and dives for sea urchins. It even got me on the Food Network! (See Taking a Dive for the Food Network, page 98.)

A few weeks before we opened The Gallery, one big challenge remained—finding local produce. I'd seen some locally grown fruits and vegetables in the tiny family-owned grocerettes, like Doi's store, where you could also get a plate lunch or a Japanese bento box with rice, pickled vegetables and raw fish. (More about the Doi's store on page 208.) But I needed restaurant quantities and much more variety. There were no farmers' markets in those days. So I instituted guerilla purchasing. We put ads in the local papers—*If you grow it, we will buy it*—asking people to contact us if they had any local produce to sell.

We also tried growing a few things ourselves. Mike Gomes, who remains a close friend, was head of the maintenance crew at the Mauna Lani resort and he helped me put in an herb garden behind the restaurant. Mike and his crew also dug an imu, a traditional Hawaiian cooking pit where we could roast a whole pig. We used the imu to create a clambake for the restaurant opening. It was a wild idea, but I had done clambakes when I worked in New England, so it felt familiar to me. We planned to serve clams, lobster, Portuguese sausage, potatoes and fresh corn—all of which would have to be brought in from the mainland. But things change, as you will see, and any cook crazy enough to do a clambake in Hawai'i today would be able to source most everything locally.

As word got around that we wanted locally grown produce, a few people showed up at the back door of the restaurant and dropped off a gift bag or two of mangos or star fruit from trees in their yards. I got lucky when I found a farmer willing to sell me fresh corn on a regular basis. His neighbor, who drove a laundry truck, agreed to deliver the

From left to right: Fred Orita, who taught me to cook octopus, make seaweed salad and much more, Tom Molelo, Tom Stoner, Brad Hirata, Peter Merriman and Sandy Barr in the kitchen at The Gallery restaurant.

corn to the restaurant, even though we didn't use that laundry service. Now that's what we call aloha spirit! Other than corn, I didn't see how we would get enough of anything we needed.

Contrary to popular opinion, there was nothing altruistic about sourcing local farm products in the 1980s. I had simply found myself on a giant island, with very few people, in the middle of the Pacific. Hotels had the benefit of huge freezers, so items shipped in could be kept for weeks. We, on the other hand, would fret over high waves on Tuesdays that could keep our weekly barge from crossing the channel and unloading at Kawaihae.

My earlier cooking experiences on the mainland and in Europe had taught me that fresh tastes better. Little by little, our passion for great tasting products led us to a breed of farmers who took tremendous pride in what they raised. At first, they didn't raise much. I bought whatever they had, and told them we were committed. If these guys would stick it out and grow more, we would buy everything they grew. We didn't have a contract or any kind of written agreement. We just trusted each other. Within a few growing seasons, the farmers had a viable cooperative going, and I had great quality produce in the quantities I needed.

I never argued about price, and to this day I don't negotiate with farmers. Whatever the farmer says it costs, we pay—I know how hard it is to grow consistently excellent produce. A rising tide raises all ships, if I'm successful, they'll be successful, too. I wanted all those farmers to be driving new trucks by the following year.

When the wine salesman stopped by with a new Cabernet for me to taste, I'd claim I was too busy and ask him to leave it on the bar; then I'd sell it by the glass later that night.

I was barely 30 years old, doing farm-to-table before anyone had coined the term, at a successful restaurant. But as you have probably figured out, I like new challenges. My wife, Vicki, and I dreamed about having our own restaurant, but we didn't have the cash to get it going. When an investor approached me and offered financing to open my own place, I jumped at it.

I wish I could say that Merriman's Waimea (still in its original location) was an instant success, but it wasn't. We opened in December 1988, in a tiny strip mall right on the main road, Route 19, about halfway between Kona and Hilo and partway up the slopes of Mauna Kea. While I cooked, Vicki did the books, ran the door, helped clean bathrooms and set tables. She always carried Cody, our first child, on her back, so I guess you could say he started in the business at just six weeks old! When my parents came to visit, they ate at the restaurant every night of their trip, trying to single-handedly put us into the black. Even with all the family help, business was agonizingly slow. I never knew if we would have enough money for the next payroll, or when the liquor purveyors might cut us off. We soon learned that business attracts business. If our restaurant had less than 50 people for the evening, I'd ask all the employees to move their cars from behind the restaurant out front to the guest parking lot. Fake it till ya make it, baby!

I have never worked harder or enjoyed it more. I kept thinking about what we could do now that we had our own restaurant, and I wanted everything to be the best. I'd brought some of the staff from The Gallery, but couldn't afford to hire many people at first so I had to do a lot of things myself. I'd show up at 7 a.m. to make fresh pasta with the hand-crank machine from our home kitchen, drying it on clothesline and broom handles strung between the pot rack and the doorjamb. I found ways to pinch pennies. When the wine salesman stopped by with a new Cabernet for me to taste, I'd claim I was too busy and ask him to leave it on the bar; then I'd sell it by the glass later that night.

Some of our thrifty ways were just a matter of survival, but some were a matter of principle. Early on at Merriman's we adopted values based on respect for the land and a philosophy of sustainability. We piled the farm boxes at the back door of the restaurant so they could be picked up and refilled by our purveyors. We did the same with plastic containers, which we sterilized in our dishwasher, a form of recycling you could never practice today. The slop was saved for the pig farmers. The motto we adopted for all Merriman's restaurants is *Do the Right Thing*—for the land, for the people of Hawai'i, and for our diners.

We barely made it the two years it took before we got our big break in Waimea. I was washing pots after lunch when one of the waiters came into the kitchen and told me a guy from *The New York Times* wanted to talk to me. *Oh great,* I thought, *some reporter wants me to comp his lunch.* I dried my hands and went into the dining room.

"Hi, I'm Peter Merriman," I said.

"I'm Johnny Apple," he replied.

I almost fell over. Johnny Apple was perhaps the best-known food writer for the *Times*.

"Welcome to Merriman's," I said, "I hope you enjoyed your lunch, and of course, it's on the house."

He said he absolutely would not accept a free meal, because if he did he couldn't write about us, and he certainly intended to write about Merriman's. It turned out he had happened in by accident. He was on vacation and driving by at lunchtime. He was impressed with

From left to right: **Paul Gamanche, general manager at Merriman's for 21 years, Vicki Merriman, Peter Merriman and T. Lowe, our son Cody's godfather.**

what we were doing—the pictures of farmers on the walls, the menu descriptions that featured the source of our ingredients, the fresh flavors, and especially the local cheese. (There are stories about these cheeses on pages 87 and 175.) I told him we used simple preparations to highlight and enhance the natural flavors. I explained how we were all about connecting the food to the land and the culture. And that's what he wrote about.

The day after the review came out, I answered the phone in the dining room. "I'll be visiting Hawaii in six weeks, and I want a reservation. Please try to fit us in," said the caller. I took his name and penciled it into the empty reservation book while assuring him that even though we were mostly booked, we would squeeze him in.

Whether it was the Johnny Apple review, or the fact that some prominent mainland chefs—like Alice Waters, Jeremiah Tower and Larry Forgione—were getting diners to think local, or both, Merriman's cuisine featuring fresh ingredients with a sense of place, became very popular, and not just with customers. Other chefs stopped in, along with resort executives, and food and beverage managers. I knew they were taking notes, but I didn't care. Now we had a following and that was just what we—both the restaurant and the farmers—needed to succeed. In fact, I started to think about ways I could get other chefs connected to the farmers.

One day in 1991, I was talking with Roger Dikon, who had recently become head chef at the Maui Prince Hotel. He and I got the idea we should get chefs from all over Hawai'i together to talk about food and cooking with local ingredients. Roger arranged for discounted accommodations at the Prince, and got us a small meeting room. We didn't really have an agenda in mind except our shared a passion for cooking the flavors of Hawai'i. Besides Roger and me, I invited 11 other chefs—Mark Ellman, a culinary pioneer on Maui; Bev Gannon, of Hali'imaile General Store on Maui; Jean-Marie Josselin, from A Pacific Café on Kauai; George Mavrothalassitis, executive chef at Halekulani Hotel in Honolulu; Amy Ota Ferguson, from Hotel Hana; Philippe Padovani, executive chef at the Ritz Carlton Mauna Lani; Gary Streuhl, from the Hawaii Prince Hotel on Waikiki; along with Alan Wong, Roy Yamaguchi and Sam Choy, all from Honolulu; and Rene Bajeux, who left for New Orleans soon after our meeting and is the often forgotten 13th chef. I asked them to come to a "symposium" (from the ancient Greek word for a meeting where there would be food and drink). Everyone accepted.

We sat around a big table in a small conference room, and I took notes. At midday we adjourned for a meal. Shep Gordon, the

To my mind, the real heroes are the farmers and ranchers, who stuck it out with us, and who face the whims of the environment every day.

Hollywood agent who would be responsible for making so many chefs into household names, was a good friend of Roger's and had invited us all to his home for lunch.

When we reconvened, we agreed to put a name to the kind of cooking we were doing, and Hawai'i Regional Cuisine (HRC) was born. It was all about the foods and flavors unique to the islands. We decided to call ourselves Hawai'i Regional Cuisine, Inc., with me as president. We also decided we should meet again soon.

Since many of the chefs didn't seem to know a lot about the local producers, I proposed we have the next meeting on the Big Island, where we could go out and meet the farmers. Somebody suggested we also invite someone from the Hawai'i Department of Agriculture (HDOA). If more chefs were going to want more local produce, we thought maybe the Ag folks could connect us with more farmers. When I called the state office, they couldn't have been more interested. Both the pineapple and sugar industries—primary sources of island income for decades—were dying out, and the Agriculture Department was looking for a way to preserve the farmland and protect it from housing developers.

Twelve of the 13 chefs (Rene had moved to the mainland by then) plus two reps from the HDOA showed up for the second meeting of HRC, Inc. We loaded everybody into the backs of three pick-up trucks and headed up the steep, pot-holed slopes of Mauna Loa. We traipsed through the rain forest, where one farmer raised parrots, to see his organic spinach. We bounced down the road to Harvey and Melissa Sacarob's lettuce farm, and stopped to see a former pakalolo farmer who now supplied me with a mix of herbs and tender sprouts that I called "salad sparkle."

HRC, Inc., went on to publish a cookbook with Janice Wald Henderson (*The New Cuisine of Hawaii,* Villard, 1994), and today Hawai'i Regional Cuisine is mainstream. Some of the chefs have moved on to other locations, or retired, but many us are still at it right here in the islands. I think it is safe to say that we are all proud of helping to create and sustain a viable agricultural community in our state. For me, it all started with a desire to serve the freshest and most flavorful food at my restaurant. The bonus was that it benefited the local economy while helping to preserve the land and the agrarian way of life. To my mind, the real heroes are the farmers, who stuck it out with us, and who face the whims of the environment every day.

I love that 20 years and eight restaurants later, my amazing staff continue to *Do the Right Thing* every single day at all our restaurants: Merriman's Waimea on the Big Island; Merriman's Kapalua, Maui; Merriman's Fish House and Merriman's Gourmet Pizza and Burgers in Poipu, Kaua'i; Merriman's Kaka'ako in Honolulu; and Monkeypod Kitchen by Merriman in Wailea, Maui; Monkeypod Ka'anapali, Maui; Monkeypod Ko'Olina, O'ahu and Moku in Honolulu, O'ahu; as well as my partnership in Hula Grill Ka'anapali, Maui. I'm always looking for ways to honor those who welcomed this East Coast haole and taught him how to cook with aloha. *Merriman's Hawai'i* is my way of saying "thank you" to all of them.

———

IN THIS BOOK, you'll find many of my favorite dishes, some from the restaurants, some from my early days of learning to cook local, and some from my personal collection. No matter where you live, these recipes will let you taste the flavors of Hawai'i—the land, the sea, the mountain ranches, and the rich cultural traditions—that make this place I call home so special to me.

CHAPTER 1

Served from the Sea: Sashimi, Poke and Shellfish

On the Origin of Recipes

I AM OFTEN ASKED how we come up with new dishes for the restaurants. The truth is that most are the result of collaboration between one or more of our chefs, me, and Merriman's Executive Chef Neil Murphy. We work with an extraordinarily talented group and we encourage creativity. Given how busy the chefs are with running the kitchens, a lot of the new ideas have to come from me. It's a little like a jazz band. I'll start playing with a few taste notes in my head—often it starts with a food memory, something memorable I ate in a little town upcountry on Maui, or across the world. I try to lay it out for one of the chefs, and he'll put it into play as a special. We tinker with it together, and if it's a hit, it goes on the menu. Sometimes one of the chefs takes the lead on some improvisation. Neil and I encourage this, as long as the new dish fits into the style of "music" we play. We want our chefs to add their own riffs, but we make sure it all stays in the right key. We never want to disguise the flavor and freshness of the food we spend so much time, energy and money to procure. Instead, we complement and accentuate the main ingredient with boldly flavored sauces and relishes.

The trick about restaurant dishes, though, is that once we get the recipe right, we have to stick with it. We have to move from improv mode to performance mode, because many diners come back for their favorites over and over again.

Every recipe in this book was tested, in most cases more than once, so if you like to play the notes as they are written, these recipes should work for you. But if you are a jazzy cook and like to improvise, I encourage you to add your own riffs and enjoy the result.

Ahi Poke

My first night in Hawai'i, the cooks from the Mauna Kea Beach Hotel brought home super-fresh ahi tuna. I couldn't believe the texture and the way it melted in my mouth—nothing like what I expected from raw fish. Nowadays there are as many recipes for poke as there are people making it. You can buy it by the pound in any deli, from supermarkets to gas stations, anywhere in the islands. This is my take on one of Hawai'i's favorite "fast" foods.

SERVES 6 TO 8 AS AN APPETIZER

POKE MARINADE

1 cup tamari
¼ cup freshly squeezed lime juice
4 large cloves garlic, minced (about 2 tablespoons)
1 (2-inch) piece fresh ginger root, peeled and minced
  (about 2 tablespoons)
5 scallions, washed and sliced into ⅛-inch rounds
  (about ¼ cup)
1½ teaspoons sambal oelek
½ cup sesame oil

PREPARE MARINADE

Place all ingredients in a blender or food processor. Puree until smooth. The marinade can be made ahead and stored for up to two weeks.

FISH

1 pound sashimi-grade ahi tuna, cut into ¾-inch dice
½ sweet onion, sliced paper thin
10 scallions, white and green parts, finely sliced
¼ cup red ogo seaweed (optional)
¼ teaspoon red pepper flakes
¾ cups Poke Marinade
¼ avocado, peeled and cut into ½-inch dice (optional)

PREPARE FISH

Place a medium bowl over ice. (Because poke is served raw, it should be kept as cold as possible both in preparation and presentation.) Add tuna, onion and scallions.

If using ogo, roughly chop while maintaining the threads and stems. Add to tuna mixture. Add chili flakes and Poke Marinade to tuna mixture. Stir together, thoroughly coating tuna in marinade and evenly blending the vegetables. Garnish with avocado, if desired, and serve immediately with sweet potato or taro chips.

Kama'aina Clams and Shrimp

Kama'aina is a Hawaiian word that means child (kama) of the land (aina). It is used to describe a person of any ancestry who was born in Hawai'i, or who has lived here for a long time. I am proud to be kama'aina. This dish is definitely a child of the islands—a combination of seafood, meat and greens as well as a mix of cultures. Be sure to have some nice crusty bread on hand to soak up the spicy, buttery broth.

SERVES 6 AS AN APPETIZER OR SERVES 3 AS A MAIN COURSE

INGREDIENTS

24 small clams, littlenecks or steamers (also known as Manila clams)
½ pound Portuguese sausage (such as linguica), sliced into ¼-inch rounds
½ onion, halved, then cut into ⅛-inch slices
6 cloves garlic, thinly sliced
6 ounces dry white wine
8 tablespoons (1 stick) butter, cut into 8 pieces
12 jumbo shrimp (U-16/20), peeled and deveined
2–3 jumbo shrimp, unpeeled (optional)
1½ cups kale, chopped
2 tablespoons olive oil
½ teaspoon red pepper flakes
Juice of ½ lemon

PREPARE CLAMS

Clean clams by placing in a large bowl and adding cold water to cover. Swirl clams in the bowl, then rub clean with your hands, letting sand and other detritus fall to the bottom. Pluck clams from the water and place in a clean, dry bowl.

COOK CLAMS

Heat a large sauté pan over high heat for 2 minutes. Add sliced sausage and brown. Add clams, onion, garlic, wine and butter. Stir, cover and cook for 3 to 5 minutes, until most of the clams open. Add peeled shrimp and unpeeled shrimp (if using), kale, olive oil and red pepper flakes. Stir well and cook, uncovered, over medium to low heat for another 30 seconds to 1 minute, until shrimp turn pink. Add lemon juice and stir.

ASSEMBLE

Serve at the table in the pan, or ladle into individual bowls.

Merriman's Fish House, Poipu, Kaua'i

Peter – this is alae rock from Kawaikaula, the next stream west from Honopue. Papa Henry Auai told me the best alae comes from Kohala Mtn. alae comes from Kohala Mtn. scrub/or scrape off the (w/H₂O) moss. a rock piece in white salt, shake to color, or powd. with a fine grater, or mix with a fine grater, or mix with liquids etc. high in iron oxide. good for blood and general tonic. The The alae is told by the between the finger tips.

Thanks for the Haleakala brke picks. You da Brke man!! Talk to me about the altitude! Aloha R. G.

Salt of the Earth

ALAEA SALT is the classic Hawaiian red salt used in cooking and in purification rituals for blessing tools, canoes, homes and temples. The distinctive color comes from red volcanic clay (alae) when it's mixed with unrefined sea salt, which is made through the evaporation of ocean water. Few people know that you can also get salt from rocks in the Kohala mountains. My buddy Rick Gordon gave me this rock and the instructions for using it—a great example of how Rick has helped connect me to some remarkable Hawaiian traditions.

Ginger-Spiked Kaua'i Shrimp

This is a gingery variation on a classic shrimp scampi—it's all about the taste of the shrimp. I think wild-caught shrimp taste best, but I also enjoy domestically raised aqua-cultured shrimp (we use fresh, Kaua'i raised). Roasted beets are a nice side dish, but in Hawai'i, you gotta have rice, so I serve both.

SERVES 4 TO 6

INGREDIENTS

½ cup olive oil

1 onion, chopped (about 1¼ cups)

4 stalks celery including leaves,
    cut in half, then cut into ¼-inch slices

1 clove garlic, peeled and minced
    (about 1 teaspoon)

6–8 plum tomatoes, chopped (seeds n' all)

1 teaspoon salt

2 pounds jumbo shrimp (U-16/20), peeled and
    deveined (I save a few unpeeled for garnish)

1 (6–8 inch) piece fresh ginger root,
    peeled and julienned (about ½ cup)

1 teaspoon sambal oelek

2 tablespoons soy sauce

PREPARE VEGETABLES

Heat a heavy skillet on high for 1 minute. Add olive oil and onion. Cook 1 minute, stirring often. Add celery and cook 1 minute more, stirring constantly. Stir in garlic. Add tomatoes and salt and reduce heat to medium. If tomatoes are very dry, add ¼ cup water. When mixture is boiling, cover, reduce heat and simmer for 5 minutes.

PREPARE SHRIMP

Uncover and increase heat to medium. Add shrimp, stir to combine and cook 1 to 2 minutes, until shrimp just starts to turn pink. Stir in ginger and sambal. Turn off heat, cover and let sit for 1 minute. Stir in soy sauce.

Keahole Lobster Mac n' Cheese

On the Big Island, near Kona, Keahole lobsters are raised in large concrete tanks of circulating, very cold sea water that's pumped up from deep in the ocean. They are fed right up until the moment they are shipped to a restaurant, which keeps them especially juicy and tender, unlike the lobsters sold in grocery stores and fish markets that may not have eaten for up to six weeks. You can use any lobster that is available to you, but if you can get Keahole, definitely go for it. Don't be afraid this dish will be too rich. The sauce, which is mostly broth and only a little cream, is lighter than you might think, and the goat cheese adds just the right tang to balance the sweetness of the lobster meat. I think this dish goes especially well with asparagus as a side, but my brother Klein says "No asparagus!" because it fights with the wine. Anyway, we agree on the best wine pairing for the dish—champagne.

SERVES 6 TO 8

LOBSTER

5–6 pounds live lobsters (4 lobsters at 1½–1¾
pounds each or 5–6 smaller lobsters)

1 to 2 quarts water

4–8 tablespoons kosher salt

MACARONI AND CHEESE

1 pound dried elbow macaroni,
fusilli or other small pasta

6 tablespoons butter

6 tablespoons all-purpose flour

4 cups chicken broth

1 cup heavy cream

¾ cup freshly grated Parmesan cheese, divided

6 tablespoons fresh (not aged) goat cheese

½ cup panko flakes or plain breadcrumbs

PREPARE LOBSTER

Many markets that sell lobsters will also cook them for you—a process they usually have down to a science. If you decide to go this route, then simply remove the cooked lobster meat as described below.

If cooking lobster yourself, you may need to do so in batches, depending on the size of your pot. For an 8-quart pot, use 1 quart water and 4 tablespoons salt; for a 16-quart pot, use 2 quarts water and 8 tablespoons salt. For a larger pot, use more water and salt. Cover the pot and bring salted water to a rolling boil. Add lobsters, head first. Use the pot lid to submerge lobsters for 1 minute. Cook for an additional 9 minutes; 7 minutes if using Keahole lobsters. Remove lobsters and allow to cool for 20 to 30 minutes.

When cool enough to handle, remove lobster meat as follows: Twist off each claw where it is attached to the body. Hold the tail in one hand, the body in the other and twist to remove the tail. Pull the fins off the end of the tail, then insert two or three fingers into the fin end of the tail and push the meat out the larger end of the tail. Use a nutcracker or lobster cracker to crack the claws and knuckles, then extract the claw and knuckle meat with a small knife or cocktail fork. Chop the meat into bite-size pieces, about ¾- to 1-inch dice. You should have 2 to 3 cups.

PREPARE MACARONI

Cook pasta according to package instructions, being careful not to overcook. Drain and transfer 8 cups (more or less, the measurement is not critical) cooked pasta to a large bowl.

PREPARE CHEESE SAUCE

Place a 4-quart saucepan over medium heat, add butter and stir occasionally. When butter is melted, stir in flour. Adjust heat so mixture just barely bubbles. Continue cooking, stirring continuously, until it turns a light tan color. Add ½ cup of the broth, whisking to dissolve any lumps, then add remaining broth and cream. Adjust heat to keep mixture at a low boil, while stirring almost constantly. The mixture will thicken slowly. When it is thick enough to coat a spoon, add ⅜ cup of the Parmesan, and all of the goat cheese. Continue stirring until mixture is slightly thicker than heavy cream. Add cheese sauce to pasta and mix thoroughly.

ASSEMBLE

Preheat the oven to 375 degrees F.

Add lobster meat to mac and cheese, mixing well. Divide mixture into 6 to 8 equal portions among individual ovenproof bowls. Sprinkle 1 tablespoon panko flakes and 1 tablespoon Parmesan cheese over each serving. Bake in the oven until bubbling and browned on top, about 10 to 15 minutes. If the top is not browned, place under the broiler for 30 seconds to 1 minute, watching carefully to avoid burning.

If you prefer to make one big casserole, transfer the lobster mixture to a casserole dish and top with ½ cup panko flakes and top with remaining Parmesan cheese, bake in the oven for 20 to 25 minutes and brown the top under the broiler (optional).

Lobsters sustainably
farmed at Kona Cold Lobsters

Lobster Papaya Daiquiri Salad

My brother Klein usually visits us for Christmas in Hawai'i. Talking about the menu for our holiday meal, he reminded me what a treat it was when we were kids to have shrimp cocktail. I had already ordered some lobsters, so I decided to make lobster daiquiri salad. Since I only needed the tails for the salad, the next day I chopped up the leftover meat with a little celery and mayonnaise and had lobster BLTs for lunch.

SERVES 6

PAPAYA SAUCE

1 ripe papaya, peeled, seeded
   and cut into ¼-inch cubes
2 tablespoons freshly squeezed lime juice
½ cup mayonnaise
1 tablespoon plus 1 teaspoon dark rum
1 teaspoon granulated sugar
⅛ teaspoon cayenne pepper
1 (½-inch) piece fresh ginger root, peeled and diced
   (about 1 teaspoon)

LOBSTER

1 quart water
4 tablespoons kosher salt
3 (1–1½-pound) live lobsters

FOR ASSEMBLY

1 head butter lettuce, leaves separated
1 cucumber, peeled, seeded and cut
   into ⅛-inch thick half-moons
1 ripe avocado, peeled, pitted and cut
   into ¼-inch dice
1 lime, cut lengthwise into 6 wedges

PREPARE SAUCE

Place papaya and lime juice in a nonreactive bowl. (If desired, set aside ½ cup for garnish.) Measure mayonnaise into a separate bowl, and add rum, sugar, cayenne and ginger. Whisk to combine, and stir in papaya and liquid. The sauce can be refrigerated for up to 2 hours.

PREPARE LOBSTER

Place water and salt in an 8-quart pot, cover and bring to a rolling boil. Add lobsters, head first. Use the pot lid to submerge lobsters for 1 minute. Cook lobsters for an additional 7 minutes for 1-pounders or 9 minutes for 1½-pounders. Remove lobsters and allow to cool for 15 to 20 minutes. When cool enough to handle, remove the tail meat by holding the body in one hand and the tail in the other, then twist and pull gently. Cut each tail (which should be nicely curved) in half lengthwise using a large French knife or cleaver, leaving the meat in the shell.

ASSEMBLE

Arrange 2 lettuce leaves on each plate, and place a half lobster tail on top, meat side up. Spoon 1½ tablespoons sauce over each serving. Arrange small servings of cucumber, avocado and papaya garnish, if using, and a lime wedge next to each lobster tail.

Merriman's Kapalua, Maui

Miso-Steamed Clams

We serve these clams in a bowl as an appetizer. You could easily turn them into a main dish by serving them over Thai-style rice noodles or pasta, like linguine or fettucine. Either way, be sure to include a big spoon. You won't want to miss a drop of the delicious broth. If you double the recipe, be sure to use a large, heavy-bottomed pot or skillet to avoid piling the clams more than two deep.

INGREDIENTS

12 littleneck or cherrystone clams, live in the shell
2 teaspoons white miso paste
2 tablespoons milk, regular or low-fat
½ teaspoon minced fresh ginger root
½ teaspoon minced fresh garlic
¼ cup onion, chopped
¼ cup celery, chopped
Pinch of cayenne pepper
½ bunch fresh kale, stemmed and large vein removed,
    sliced laterally into 1-inch strips (about 2 cups)
1 tablespoon mirin
2 tablespoons unsalted butter

PREPARE CLAMS

Follow cleaning method described on page 31.

PREPARE BROTH

Place white miso paste and milk in an unheated sauté pan and stir to combine. Bring mixture to a low boil over medium-high heat. Add ginger, garlic, onion, celery and cayenne pepper, and stir to combine. Bring mixture back to a low boil. Add kale, stir and cook until kale just begin to wilt.

FINISH CLAMS

Add clams, cover and place over high heat, about 3 minutes, until all clams are open.

After clams have opened, reduce heat to medium. (Don't be concerned if the milk looks curdled; it will come back together when you add the butter.) Using tongs or a slotted spoon, remove clams and kale to a serving bowl.

FINISH BROTH

With the pan still on medium heat, stir in mirin, whisk in butter and continue whisking until the broth is smooth and homogeneous, about 1 minute.

ASSEMBLE

Pour broth over clams and serve immediately.

Poisson Cru

I learned the secret to great poisson cru from Auntie Ilima. I met her in the early days of Merriman's Waimea. "You gotta salt the fish first," she said, "That's how we do it in Tahiti." She's right. It makes sense that the salt brines the fish before you add the citrus, so as it "cooks" in the acid it gets super tender. Ono is also known as wahoo throughout the islands and is related to the king mackerel. This is one of my son Cody's favorites.

SERVES 6 AS AN APPETIZER

FISH

1 pound ono

2 teaspoons Hawaiian salt or kosher salt
  or coarse sea salt

½ cup freshly squeezed lime juice

½ cup canned unsweetened coconut milk, shaken
  or stirred to reincorporate the separated cream

¼ sweet onion, diced (about ¼ cup)

1 small tomato, cored, seeded,
  cut into ¼-inch dice and drained

¼–½ seedless cucumber,
  peeled and cut into ¼-inch dice

½ small jalapeño pepper, seeded and minced

FOR ASSEMBLY

6 leaves butter lettuce

3 scallions, green part only, cut into ¼-inch slices

PREPARE FISH

Remove skin and dark meat from the fish and cut remaining white meat into a ½-inch dice. Place in a stainless steel or glass bowl and sprinkle with salt. Using a spoon or spatula, gently toss fish by scooping and turning over in a folding motion. Cover with plastic wrap and let sit for 30 minutes at room temperature. Add lime juice and toss gently to distribute evenly over the fish. Cover with plastic wrap and marinate in the refrigerator for 1 to 4 hours. (The longer it marinates, the stronger the lime flavor.)

Remove fish from the refrigerator and drain 90 percent of the lime juice. Add coconut milk, onion, tomato, cucumber and jalapeño pepper. Cover and chill for at least 30 minutes, and up to 24 hours.

ASSEMBLE

Arrange lettuce leaves among 6 plates. Divide and distribute fish, garnishing with scallions.

Shrimp Luau

The Hawaiian word luau means taro leaf and was not used to describe a feast until after European contact. Throughout the islands, you will see variations of this traditional soup using chicken, shrimp or squid. In this version, I have substituted spinach for the more historically authentic taro leaf as it is easier to find and still delicious. Although the photo shows whole shrimp, I prefer them peeled and deveined—makes it easier to enjoy a bite with all the flavors combined.

SERVES 6 AS AN APPETIZER OR SERVES 3 AS A MAIN COURSE

INGREDIENTS
2 cups onions, chopped
1 (13–15-ounce) can coconut milk
1 tablespoon nam pla
6 ($^1\!/_4$-inch) slices peeled fresh ginger root
12 jumbo shrimp (U-16/20), peeled and deveined
8 ounces fresh spinach or baby spinach, stemmed and leaves
*   cut into 1-inch strips*
2 teaspoons anise-flavored liqueur (such as Pernod, Sambuca or Ouzo)
$^1\!/_4$ teaspoon cayenne pepper
$^1\!/_2$ teaspoon salt

PREPARE SOUP
In a large saucepan, combine onions, coconut milk, nam pla and ginger. Bring to a simmer over medium-high heat. Reduce heat, cover and continue simmering for 30 minutes. Add shrimp and simmer another 2 minutes, stirring occasionally. Add spinach, liqueur, cayenne and salt. Stir to combine and simmer 2 minutes more. Before serving, remove ginger slices.

Shrimp and Corn Fritters with Roasted Poblano Sour Cream

We serve these fritters on a platter with a dipping sauce made with roasted poblano peppers and sour cream. You can make them smaller for a passed hors d'oeuvre. Larger fritters are delicious on a green salad for lunch, or dinner.

MAKES 24 FRITTERS

FRITTERS

2 small ears fresh corn

10 scallions, coarsely chopped (about ²/₃ cup)

2 medium carrots, peeled and chopped
    into ¼-inch dice

1 stalk celery, chopped into ¼-inch dice
    (about ¹/₃ cup)

2 large cloves garlic, minced
    (about 1 tablespoon)

2 shallots, chopped (about 2 tablespoons)

1 (3-inch) piece fresh ginger root,
    peeled and minced (about 3 tablespoons)

¼ teaspoon red pepper flakes

1 teaspoon ground cumin

¼ teaspoon kosher salt

¼ cup vegetable oil, divided

2 pounds shrimp, peeled and deveined, divided

1 cup roasted, salted macadamia nuts,
    coarsely chopped

Roasted Poblano Sour Cream
    (page 52)

PREPARE FRITTERS

Cut corn kernels from cobs and set aside; you should have about 1 cup.

Place scallions, carrot, celery, garlic, shallots, ginger, red pepper flakes, cumin, salt and 1 teaspoon of the oil in a food processor. Chop with 6 pulses, scrape the sides clean, chop for another 5 seconds, scrape the sides clean, and chop continuously for 5 seconds more, until all vegetables are in very small pieces. Add one-quarter of the shrimp to vegetable mixture. Puree continuously for 15 seconds, scrape the sides clean, then puree 15 seconds more. Add corn and macadamia nuts. Pulse 8 to 10 times until nuts are well broken up. Remove mixture and place in a large bowl.

Place remaining shrimp in the food processor; pulse 4 times to break shrimp into smaller pieces, scrape the sides clean, then pulse 4 times more. Add to pureed shrimp and vegetable mixture. Fold all ingredients together until well mixed.

Add 1 tablespoon oil to a large nonstick skillet; turn heat to medium-high and heat oil for 30 seconds. Using a measuring cup, add about ¼ cup of the fritter mixture to the skillet and flatten slightly. Continue adding fritters, but do not let them touch. Cook for 1 to 2 minutes, until well browned, then turn over and cook another 1 to 2 minutes; the shrimp will be pink. Remove fritters to a plate lined with a double thickness of paper towels to drain excess oil. Continue cooking fritters in batches.

Recipe continued on page 52

Roasted Poblano Sour Cream

This roasted pepper cream has a nice little bite, which can be adjusted by adding more or less jalapeño pepper. It's the perfect dipping sauce for shrimp fritters, and I also like to use it in fish tacos.

MAKES 3 CUPS

INGREDIENTS

3 poblano peppers

1 jalapeño pepper

1 bunch fresh cilantro

2 medium cloves garlic, minced
   (about 1 tablespoon)

1 tablespoon freshly squeezed lime juice

2 cups sour cream

1 teaspoon ground cumin

½ teaspoon salt

⅛ teaspoon freshly ground black pepper

PREPARATION

Roast poblano and jalapeño peppers over an open flame until charred. Place charred peppers in a paper bag, or wrap in plastic wrap for 5 minutes to sweat them, then peel (scraping with the back edge of a knife) the charred skin; remove seeds and chop peppers into ½-inch squares. Separate cilantro stems and leaves; chop stems very fine, then coarsely chop leaves.

Combine peppers, cilantro, garlic, lime juice, sour cream, cumin, salt and pepper in a blender or food processor and puree until smooth.

THE CHEF'S KNIFE is a cook's primary tool. Regardless of how many other knives we have, most use the chef's knife about 90 percent of the time. My first chef's knife was given to me by Chef Hans Schadler in 1978. I had done my apprenticeship under Chef Schadler at the Rock-Resorts. I spent most of those two and a half years in Woodstock, Vermont, with one summer in Grand Teton National Park learning to butcher.

Earlier in 1978, I was working as a restaurant manager at the World Trade Center in New York trying to decide whether to stay in management or start all over as a cook's apprentice. I sought the advice of Jerry Green, who was the sous chef at the Market Bar where I worked. His response was simple but sparked an epiphany for me that I'll never forget.

"Pete," Jerry said, "The thing about cookin,' is ya got a trade you walk with." Not quite following, I asked for more details. He said, "It's like being a guitar player. You can work wherever you like. Everyone needs good cooks."

The sharpening marks on the blade bear witness to a knife that has traveled from Martha's Vineyard, to Frankfurt, Germany, to the Big Island, and now, Maui. I still use it today but not as often. That knife was my guitar. It allowed me to walk all over, and end up in Hawai'i.

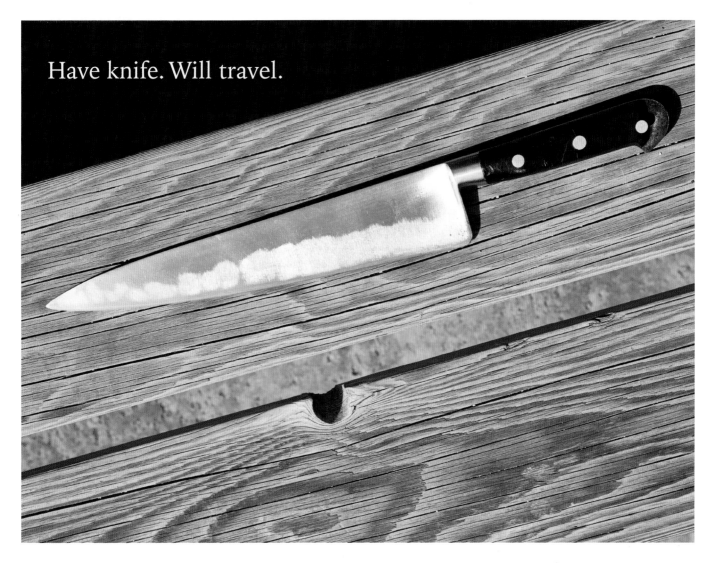

Have knife. Will travel.

Shrimp Broccoli

This is a popular local dish you'll find in many casual diners and restaurants all over the islands. Even though it is cooked by stirring while sautéing, it is not a typical stir-fry with a soy-based sauce. Instead, it is fairly dry and highly spiced. I love how this simple prep delivers a ton of flavor. Peeling and deveining the shrimp before cooking makes them easier to enjoy. And, of course, I serve it with some rice.

SERVES 4

STIR-FRY

2 egg whites
2 tablespoons cornstarch
1 teaspoon salt, divided
⅛ teaspoon freshly ground black pepper
8 tablespoons canola oil, divided
16 colossal shrimp (U-15), peeled and deveined
1–2 crowns broccoli
⅜ cup water
6 cloves garlic, finely chopped
1 (½-inch) piece fresh ginger root, peeled and minced
½ teaspoon red pepper flakes
¼ sweet onion, very thinly sliced
1½ teaspoons soy sauce

PREPARE SHRIMP

Place egg whites, cornstarch, ½ teaspoon of the salt, black pepper and 2 tablespoons of the canola oil in a large bowl. Whisk until combined. Add shrimp and stir gently to coat well. Let sit for 5 minutes, stirring once or twice.

PREPARE BROCCOLI

While shrimp are resting, cut broccoli (florets only) into pieces no bigger than the size of a quarter, leaving about ½-inch of stem attached. You should have about 1½ cups of florets.

STIR-FRY

Heat 6 tablespoons canola oil in a wok or large skillet over high heat for 30 seconds. Using tongs, pluck shrimp from the liquid and place in the pan, being careful to avoid hot spattering oil. Add broccoli and sauté 1 minute, stirring often. The broccoli should brown a little, and the shrimp should start to turn pink. Add water and continue cooking, stirring occasionally, until broccoli is bright green and just tender. Reduce heat to medium and add garlic, ginger, red pepper flakes and remaining ½ teaspoon salt. Cook, stirring occasionally, for 1 to 2 minutes more.

ASSEMBLE

Transfer cooked shrimp and broccoli to a serving bowl or platter. Top with sweet onion and drizzle soy sauce over all.

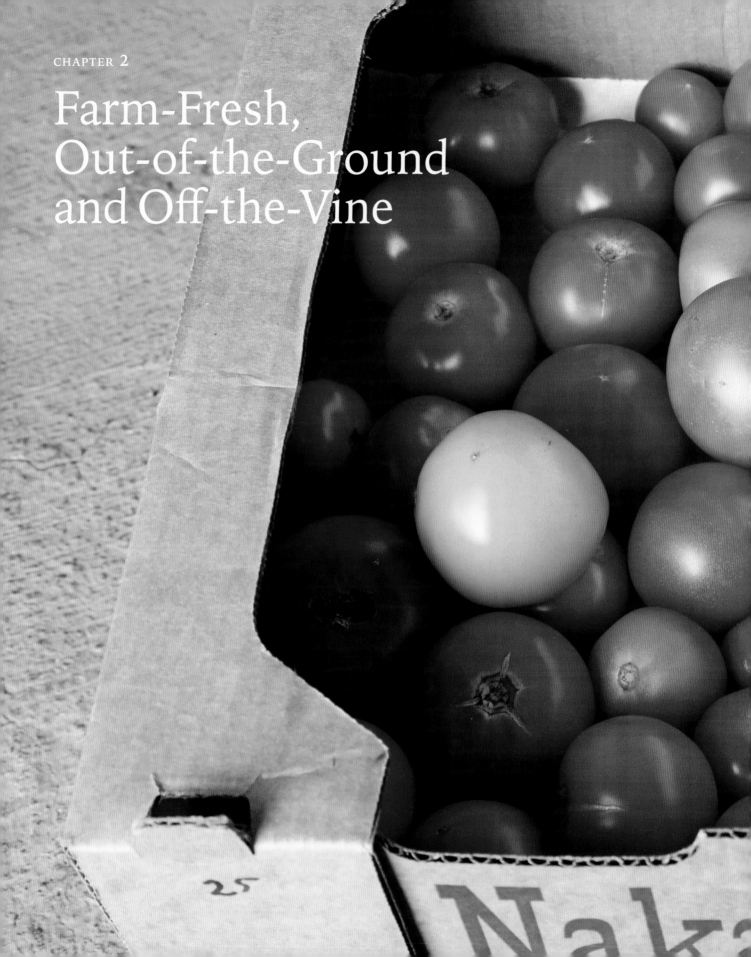

CHAPTER 2

Farm-Fresh,
Out-of-the-Ground
and Off-the-Vine

Chef Neil Murphy

WHEN OUR FIRST EXECUTIVE CHEF left Merriman's in 2005, I activated the chef telephone and email tree. Soon, I heard about Neil Murphy from several colleagues. Neil was cooking in New York City, and he had let it be known he would love to move someplace new and different. I asked why I had never heard of him. The answer was always some variation on the same theme—Neil is the best cook in the city, but he doesn't like to play the media game.

Once we got on the phone, it turned out Neil knew a lot about me. He had eaten at Merriman's Waimea during his recent vacation—and he loved the idea of living in Hawai'i. I asked him about his goals. "Hey, all I want to do is cook. I just love to cook, man." He was speaking my language, so I hired him then and there. Once he arrived on the Big Island, I saw firsthand his dedication to and appreciation for high quality ingredients along with his disciplined cooking technique. In less than a month, he took over as chef at Merriman's Waimea. Six years later,

Neil became executive chef overseeing the kitchens in all of the Merriman's and Monkeypod Kitchen by Merriman restaurants.

Chef Neil Murphy has left his mark all over this cookbook. Every dish photographed for this book was prepared and plated under his watchful eye, if not by his own talented hands. And many of the recipes were originally his idea, including Lobster Papaya Daiquiri Salad (page 40) and Smoked Taro Hummus (page 95).

If you can find a video or rerun of the Merriman's Fish House episode on the Food Network show *Chef Hunter*, you can see Chef Neil in action in the kitchen. Big talent, great fun!

Spicy Greens with Grilled Pineapple

Grilled pineapple is a fairly common dessert in Hawai'i. I wanted to feature it at the beginning of the meal so I created this marinade, which highlights the sweetness without boosting it. The greens have just the right amount of bite to offset the pineapple, making this a wonderful appetizer or the perfect side dish to accompany grilled shrimp, fish or chicken. I like to serve it with Macadamia Nut–Crusted Ono (page 112).

SERVES 6

GRILLED PINEAPPLE
1 fresh pineapple, peeled and cored
4 tablespoons brown sugar
2 tablespoons salt
½ teaspoon freshly ground black pepper
1 teaspoon soy sauce
3 tablespoons freshly squeezed lime juice
½ cup canola oil

PREPARE AND MARINATE PINEAPPLE
Cut the cored, peeled pineapple lengthwise into sixths and place pineapple wedges in a shallow baking dish.

Measure brown sugar, salt, pepper, soy sauce, lime juice and canola oil into a small bowl. Whisk to combine. Pour marinade over the pineapple, cover with plastic wrap and marinate for 30 minutes to 1 hour, turning it once or twice.

GRILL PINEAPPLE
Prepare a charcoal or gas grill, and preheat the grill rack for at least 5 minutes. Place pineapple slices on the grill and cook for 5 to 7 minutes, until lightly browned, basting with marinade once after 3 minutes. Turn the pineapple and cook for another 5 to 7 minutes, until lightly browned, basting once more after 3 minutes. Remove pineapple from the grill and distribute among 6 serving plates. If you prefer a tossed salad, chop the pineapple into cubes.

SPICY GREENS
2 ounces arugula
2 ounces watercress
2 ounces baby mustard greens or turnip greens or kale (but not baby kale)

DRESSING
¼ cup freshly squeezed lime juice
⅜ cup extra-virgin olive oil
2 teaspoons soy sauce
¼ teaspoon kosher salt

PREPARE GREENS AND DRESSING
Place the greens in a large bowl.

Measure lime juice, olive oil, soy sauce and salt into a separate bowl. Whisk well to thoroughly combine.

Pour half the dressing over the greens and toss well. If making a composed salad, divide greens into equal portions next to pineapple wedges; drizzle 1 to 2 teaspoons dressing over each serving. If making a tossed salad, add pineapple to the dressed greens and toss. Remaining dressing can be passed at the table.

Moloka'i Sweet Potato Palau

Palau is the Hawaiian name of a pudding made with sweet potatoes and coconut cream. Moloka'i sweet potatoes are purple, but you can substitute the more commonly available orange variety. The dish is not overly sweet, and I like to serve it with fish with Spicy Liliko'i Sauce (page 118), or a simple ham dish, or any of the spicier fish preparations.

SERVES 8 TO 10 AS A SIDE DISH

PALAU

3 large purple Moloka'i sweet potatoes
   (about 2 pounds) or orange sweet potatoes
1/2 cup plus 1 tablespoon butter, divided
1 onion, diced (about 1 cup)
1 cup canned unsweetened coconut milk
1 teaspoon salt
1 tablespoon chopped scallions,
   green parts only, for garnish
3 cloves garlic, sliced and fried
   in 1 tablespoon canola oil, for garnish

PREPARE SWEET POTATOES

Peel and cut sweet potatoes into 2-inch cubes. Place in a 4-quart saucepan with lid and add water until potatoes are just covered. Bring to a boil, cover and simmer, partially covered, for 10 to 15 minutes, until potatoes are easily pierced with a sharp knife. Do not overcook.

PREPARE ONION

While the potatoes are cooking, melt 1 tablespoon of the butter in a skillet over medium heat. Add onion and sauté, stirring often, until translucent, but not browned. Remove from heat and set aside.

PREPARE PALAU

Drain potatoes in a colander. Melt remaining butter in a 4-quart saucepan over medium-low heat. Add potatoes and stir gently to coat with melted butter. The potatoes will fall apart as they cook, releasing liquid that should evaporate as they continue to cook, 5 to 10 minutes, with gentle stirring. When no more liquid is released, remove from heat and set aside.

ASSEMBLE

Add coconut milk and mash the potatoes by stirring vigorously, or whipping until smooth. Stir in sautéed onions and salt. Transfer palau to a serving bowl and garnish with scallions and fried garlic.

Erin Lee and the Birth of an Industry

IN 1987, The Gallery restaurant had been open for about a year. It was gaining attention across the state as the place with a horrible location and lots of customers, because we served locally sourced food. The back door of the kitchen opened one day, and a woman walked in with a basket full of beautiful herbs. It was Erin Lee and little did I know that she would soon change Hawai'i agriculture forever.

At the time, it was well known that vine-ripened tomatoes would not grow in Hawai'i. The fruit flies stung them at lower elevations, and too much rain fell on the upper slopes. I told Erin that day, "We have enough herbs. What we're looking for is vine-ripened tomatoes." I suspected that might be the last

I would see of her, until four months later when she walked back in the same door carrying that same basket. This time it was filled with exactly what I needed: gorgeous vine-ripened tomatoes.

How did Erin accomplish the unimaginable? Well, Erin's not your average grower. She used her huge intellect to determine that if she built a greenhouse on the upper slopes of the rainforest, and then irrigated inside, it would solve the vine-ripe issue. Lokelani tomatoes, named for Erin's farm, Lokelani Gardens, became a signature item on the Merriman's menu.

Erin did a lot more than make me look good. About the same time she was demonstrating an efficient production method for vine-ripes, the Big Island's cut-flower farmers came under threat. In addition to battling the usual diseases, Waimea's export flower industry began to face serious competition from South America. The shift from carnations to tomatoes was relatively easy, and many farmers were able to stay solvent. Today, Waimea tomatoes can be found on menus across the island chain.

Ricotta Cavatelli Pasta with Asparagus and Mushrooms

If you've never made hand-rolled pasta, this is the recipe for you. Okay, so maybe these aren't really authentic cavatelli. We skip the little rolling motion, and just cut the dough into strips—so easy, and they taste amazing. Go ahead and try it. The rest of the preparation is simple but takes some time. You will be rewarded with a deeply flavorful bowl of pasta and veggies—a meal in itself—or wonderful with some grilled chicken.

Merriman's Fish House, Poipu, Kaua'i

PASTA

1 egg
1 cup ricotta cheese
1¾ cups all-purpose flour, plus extra for rolling out pasta dough
4 quarts water

PREPARE CAVATELLI PASTA

Place eggs, ricotta and flour into a large bowl and knead by hand until well mixed. Sprinkle flour on a cutting board or clean counter and roll out one-quarter of the dough into a rectangle ⅛-inch thick. Cut pasta dough into 1½-inch strips, then cut across each strip at ¼-inch intervals to make pieces 1½-inch long, ¼-inch wide and ⅛-inch thick. Continue rolling out and cutting pasta dough as described.

In a large pot, bring water to a boil; near the stovetop, place a large bowl filled with ice water.

COOK PASTA

Place pasta into boiling water and stir gently. Blanch for 2 minutes, then drain in a colander or remove with a slotted spoon or hand strainer, and plunge into ice-water bath to stop pasta from further cooking. Blanched pasta can be stored in the refrigerator for up to 2 days.

MUSHROOMS

3 tablespoons soy sauce
1 tablespoon sake or white wine
2 tablespoons canola oil
1 teaspoon kosher salt
¼ teaspoon freshly ground black pepper
8 ounces cremini mushrooms, sliced ¼-inch thick
¼ onion, thinly sliced
2 cloves garlic, thinly sliced
1 tablespoon butter, melted

ROAST MUSHROOMS

Preheat the oven to 425 degrees F, using a roast setting, if available. Place soy sauce, sake, oil, salt and pepper into a bowl and whisk to combine. Add mushrooms, onion, and garlic, then add melted butter. Toss gently to combine. Spread mixture onto a baking sheet. Roast for 12 minutes, check, and if not well browned, roast for 3 to 5 minutes more. Set aside until ready for assembly.

Recipe continued on page 68

Recipe continued from page 67

ASPARAGUS

8 spears asparagus

2 tablespoons canola oil

½ teaspoon salt

⅛ teaspoon freshly ground black pepper

SAUTÉ ASPARAGUS

Trim asparagus and cut spears into ¾-inch pieces. Heat a sauté pan over medium-high heat for 1 minute. Add canola oil, heat 30 seconds, and add asparagus. Sauté for 1 minute, add salt and pepper and sauté another 30 seconds. Remove asparagus to a bowl and set aside until ready for assembly.

FOR ASSEMBLY

1 cup chicken stock

4 tablespoons unsalted butter, cut into 4 pieces

Roasted Mushrooms

4 cups blanched Ricotta Cavatelli Pasta

Sautéed Asparagus

½ cup freshly grated Parmesan cheese

½ cup ricotta cheese

¼ cup fresh parsley, chopped

In a skillet, bring chicken stock to a boil and continue boiling for 30 seconds to reduce slightly. Whisk in butter, 1 piece at a time. Add mushrooms and cavatelli. Stir and cook over medium-high heat, until the liquid begins to thicken, about 1 to 2 minutes. Add asparagus and Parmesan cheese. Stir well to combine.

ASSEMBLE

Divide pasta among 4 bowls. Top each serving with 2 tablespoons ricotta cheese and 1 tablespoon parsley.

Merriman's Signature Pineapple Cole Slaw

This Asian-style cabbage salad is sweet and sour, salty and spicy. It's very different from the familiar creamy American-style slaw—in a good way. It's deliciously refreshing with Chinese-Style Braised Beef Short Ribs (page 140) or Kalua Pork (page 164), and I love adding it to a ham sandwich.

SERVES 8 TO 10 AS A SIDE DISH

SLAW

½ head Napa cabbage, cored, quartered
    and sliced into ¼-inch ribbons
⅛ head red cabbage,
    cored and sliced into ¼-inch ribbons
½ red onion, halved and sliced with the grain
    (not across) into ⅛-inch julienne
3 scallions, green parts only,
    sliced into ¼-inch lengths
2 large radishes, cut into ⅛-inch-thick sticks
1 recipe Cole Slaw Dressing

FOR ASSEMBLY

1 fresh pineapple, cut into ½-inch cubes
    (about 2 cups)
2 tablespoons toasted sesame seeds
    (page 83 for toasting directions)
¼ cup bean sprouts

DRESSING

2½ tablespoons champagne vinegar
¼ cup rice wine vinegar
¼ cup granulated sugar
2½ tablespoons soy sauce
1 (½-inch) piece fresh ginger root, peeled and finely chopped
    (about ½ tablespoon)
¼ cup toasted sesame oil
2½ tablespoons nam pla or nuoc mam
Pinch of cayenne pepper
2 teaspoons kosher salt or coarse salt

PREPARE DRESSING

Place all ingredients in a medium bowl and whisk until well combined.

PREPARE SLAW

Place both cabbages, onion, scallions and radishes in a large bowl and toss well. Add ½ cup of the dressing and toss until well combined. The slaw can be made ahead and stored in the refrigerator for up to 4 hours.

ASSEMBLE

Just before serving, drain any accumulated juice from the cut pineapple (drink the juice if you like, that's what I do). Add pineapple, sesame seeds and bean sprouts to the slaw mixture. Toss well. Taste and add more dressing, as desired.

From left to right: The Mount Rushmore of Hawai'i farmers and me: Erin Lee, Kurt Hirabara, Richard Ha, Ken Hufford, Peter Merriman and Tane Datta.

Kenneth Rambayon,
sous chef at
Merriman's Waimea.

Coconut Squash Chowder

Kabocha squash is a staple of Thai cooking. It looks like a small, dark green pumpkin. In mainland markets, you may find it labeled buttercup (as distinguished from butternut, which is tan and shaped like a fat bowling pin and which can be used instead if kabocha is unavailable). Like most winter squashes, kabocha has a thick, hard skin. The suggested method for liberating the flesh: Cut the squash in half from top to bottom; scoop out the seeds; slice one or both halves into wedges; and cut the flesh away into chunks. This vegetarian chowder is a variation on Coconut Fish Chowder (page 100). I like it super spicy, but you can temper the heat for more delicate palates by cutting back on the sambal or removing the seeds from the Thai chili before slicing.

SERVES 8 AS A SIDE DISH OR APPETIZER, OR SERVES 4 AS A MAIN COURSE

CHOWDER

2 tablespoons vegetable oil or coconut oil

1 sweet onion, diced (about 1 cup)

2 stalks lemongrass, white part only,
    cut lengthwise into quarters then minced
    (about ¼ cup)

2 cups chicken stock or vegetable stock

1 (1-inch) piece fresh galangal or 1 (1½-inch)
    piece fresh ginger root, minced
    (about 1½ tablespoons)

2 tablespoons nuoc mam or nam pla

1 teaspoon sambal oelek or 1 fresh Thai chili,
    cut into ⅛-inch rounds

1½ cups canned unsweetened coconut milk

½ large (about 1½-pound) kabocha squash
    or 1 small butternut squash, peeled,
    seeded and cut into 1-inch pieces

FOR ASSEMBLY

4 kaffir lime leaves (optional)

1 cup bean sprouts

½ cup roasted, unsalted peanuts or cashews

¼ cup fresh mint leaves or fresh Thai basil leaves

PREPARE SQUASH

Heat a nonstick sauté pan over high heat for 1 minute. Add oil and swirl to distribute evenly. Add onion and cook until soft, but not browned. Add lemongrass, stir and continue cooking 1 minute. Add stock, stir well and bring to a boil. Reduce heat to medium-low and simmer for 3 minutes. Add galangal, nuoc mam and coconut milk, and stir. Add squash and bring to a boil, then reduce heat and simmer, uncovered, for 12 to 15 minutes. The squash should be just tender (easily pierced with a sharp knife) but still firm. Serve immediately or chill in a covered container for up to 48 hours. Reheat prior to serving, but do not allow chowder to boil.

ASSEMBLE

Remove from heat. If using, roll kaffir lime leaves between your fingers to bruise them. Add to the chowder and stir. Ladle chowder into bowls and garnish with bean sprouts, nuts and mint. *Kaffir lime leaves are not edible, so tell diners to remove them.*

Garden Stir-Fry with Chinese Black Bean Sauce

These are not the black beans typically used in Mexican or Cuban cooking. Chinese black beans are actually soybeans that have been dried and fermented with salt and maybe some other spices like chilies or ginger. They are also called salted or dried black beans and can be found in many Asian groceries. The recipe makes twice as much sauce as you'll need. Use the rest to enhance a plain chicken breast or some steamed clams. Feel free to vary the vegetables in the garden stir-fry, using whatever you like best that is super fresh.

SERVES 4

GARDEN STIR-FRY

2 tablespoons canola or peanut oil
1 cup broccoli florets with 1-inch stems
½ cup carrots, peeled and cut into ¼-inch pieces
½ cup bamboo shoots or Jerusalem artichokes, matchstick cut
½ cup Anaheim or banana peppers, matchstick cut
½ sweet onion, julienned
1 cup fresh mushrooms (any variety), sliced
¾ cup snap peas or snow peas
2 heads baby bok choy, cut lengthwise into 4 pieces
4 cloves garlic, thinly sliced
1 (1-inch) piece fresh ginger root, peeled and matchstick cut
1 teaspoon salt
¼ teaspoon red pepper flakes
1 cup Chinese Black Bean Sauce, at room temperature
White or brown rice
3–4 scallions, white and green parts, cut into ½-inch pieces (about ¼ cup)

PREPARE STIR-FRY

Heat a wok or large sauté pan on high for 1 minute. Add oil and heat for 20 to 30 seconds, until shimmering. Add all vegetables, except scallions and stir-fry for approximately 3 minutes. Add salt and red pepper flakes. Stir-fry another minute. Add 1 cup Black Bean Sauce and stir well to coat vegetables. Immediately remove from heat. Serve over white or brown rice, and top with sliced green onions.

Chinese Black Bean Sauce

MAKES ABOUT 2 CUPS

INGREDIENTS

1 cup fermented black beans
¼ cup sugar
5 tablespoons soy sauce
¼ cup mirin
2 large cloves garlic, minced (about 2 tablespoons)
1 (1-inch) piece fresh ginger root, peeled and minced (about 1 tablespoon)
1½ tablespoons cornstarch mixed with 1 tablespoon cold water

PREPARE SAUCE

Place black beans in a mesh strainer and rinse thoroughly under cold running water. In a stainless steel pot, stir together beans, sugar, soy sauce, mirin, garlic and ginger. Add enough water to cover beans by ½ inch. Bring to a low boil, then simmer, uncovered, for 5 minutes. Swirl or stir cornstarch slurry and add to the beans. Stir until thickened. Sauce can be used immediately or cooled and refrigerated for up to 3 weeks.

Golden Salad—Beets, Tomatoes and Papaya

Unless you are lucky enough to live in Hawai'i, or maybe Florida, this is a summer salad. Don't even try to make it unless you can get really good tomatoes, and a nice ripe papaya. The vinaigrette has just a touch of heat to highlight the sweetness of the beets and papaya.

Marie-Rose Nakano

SERVES 4 TO 6 AS A SIDE DISH OR SERVES 2 TO 3 FOR LUNCH

BEETS AND QUINOA

3 golden beets, peeled

1 tablespoon olive oil

1½ teaspoons salt, divided

⅛ teaspoon freshly ground black pepper

½ cup water

¼ cup red or black quinoa

DRESSING

¼ cup freshly squeezed lime juice

¼ cup champagne vinegar

1 tablespoon Dijon mustard

½ teaspoon salt

⅛ teaspoon freshly ground black pepper

½ teaspoon red pepper flakes

1 tablespoon chopped fresh flat-leaf parsley,
    leaves only

¾ cup extra-virgin olive oil

FOR ASSEMBLY

2 large ripe tomatoes,
    cored and cut into ¼-inch slices

1 red onion, diced

1 ripe papaya, peeled and cut into ½-inch dice

5–6 fresh basil leaves

PREPARE BEETS

Preheat the oven to 375 degrees F.

Rub beets with olive oil and season with 1 teaspoon of the salt and ⅛ teaspoon of the pepper. Place beets in a small roasting pan, cover the pan with foil, and roast for 45 minutes. When cool, cut beets into a rustic ¾-inch dice. Set aside.

PREPARE QUINOA

Place water and remaining salt into a saucepan, bring to a boil, add quinoa and stir to combine. Cover and simmer for 30 minutes or more, until the grain is tender. Drain well and set aside.

PREPARE DRESSING

Place lime juice, vinegar, mustard, salt, pepper, red pepper flakes and parsley into a small bowl and whisk to combine. Drizzle in olive oil, whisking continuously.

ASSEMBLE

Arrange tomatoes on a platter. Top each tomato with a small portion of the diced beets, onions, papaya and quinoa. Drizzle vinaigrette over all and garnish with fresh basil.

Spinach Quinoa Salad

This super light vegetarian salad is also extra healthy because of the protein in the quinoa. It makes a wonderful lunch or dinner entree, but I also like to serve it as a side dish when I barbeque at home. At the restaurant, we shave the Maui onion on top. If you prefer, chop it and mix it into the salad.

Kurt Hirabara on his farm in Waimea

SERVES 4 AS A SIDE DISH OR SERVES 2 AS A MAIN COURSE

SALAD

2 ears corn, husks on

1 cup quinoa

2 cups boiling water

3 large or 5 small radishes, thinly sliced

½ large cucumber, halved or quartered lengthwise and thinly sliced

1 medium tomato, diced

3 pieces hearts of palm, cut in half lengthwise and thinly sliced (about ½ cup)

1 tablespoon chopped fresh mint

1 tablespoon chopped fresh basil

1 tablespoon chopped fresh cilantro

1 teaspoon table salt

¼ teaspoon freshly ground black pepper

1 teaspoon freshly squeezed lemon juice

¼ cup Miso-Sesame Vinaigrette (page 82)

5 ounces baby spinach

¼ sweet onion, very thinly sliced

PREPARE CORN

Grill corn in their husks over a charcoal fire for 10 minutes, turning frequently, or coat shucked corn with olive oil and roast for 10 minutes in the oven preheated to 400 degrees F. When corn is cool enough to handle, cut kernels from cob and place in a small bowl.

PREPARE QUINOA

In a dry 2-quart saucepan over medium heat, toast quinoa until fragrant and just barely turning tan. Add boiling water, stir, cover and set aside for 5 minutes. Fluff quinoa with a fork and transfer to a large bowl. Set aside to cool for 10 minutes.

ASSEMBLE

Add corn kernels, radishes, cucumber, tomato, hearts of palm, mint, basil and cilantro to quinoa and mix well. Add salt, pepper, lemon juice and Miso-Sesame Vinaigrette and mix. Add spinach and toss gently but thoroughly. Before plating, taste and add more vinaigrette, if needed. Top with sweet onion.

Hamakua Miso Mushrooms

For this recipe, I like to use alii mushrooms from Hamakua Heritage Farms on the Big Island. Unlike most other mushrooms, even the stems are flavorful and have a meaty texture. They look like something out of a Dr. Seuss story! You can find them in specialty markets, even on the East Coast, but you can also substitute oyster, cremini or any firm wild mushroom. Serve them over steak, chicken, fish, or mixed into pasta.

MAKES 6 SERVINGS AS A TOPPING OR MAKES 2 SERVINGS FOR PASTA

INGREDIENTS

¼ cup olive oil
8 ounces fresh mushrooms, sliced lengthwise into ³/₈-inch-thick pieces
2 large cloves garlic, minced (about 1 tablespoon)
1 (¾-inch) piece fresh ginger root, peeled and minced (about 2 teaspoons)
¼ cup dry white wine
2 tablespoons white or red miso paste
2 tablespoons unsalted butter
1 tablespoon soy sauce
¼ teaspoon freshly ground black pepper
²/₃ cup fresh flat-leaf parsley, leaves only, or 4 scallions, green parts only,
    cut into ¼-inch slices

PREPARATION

Heat a nonstick skillet over high heat for 30 seconds. Add olive oil, immediately add mushrooms and stir to coat with oil. Reduce heat slightly and cook for 1 minute, stirring continuously, until mushrooms just begin to soften. Add garlic and ginger, stir and cook 1 minute more. Add wine and stir to combine. Add miso and stir well, then add butter, 1 tablespoon at a time, stirring continuously. Turn off heat as soon as the butter melts. Add soy sauce and pepper, and stir well. Taste, and adjust saltiness by adding a little more soy sauce, if needed. Garnish with parsley.

Monkeypod Kitchen Kale Salad with Miso-Sesame Vinaigrette

Everybody thinks it's the macadamia nuts that give this salad its unique taste of the islands, but it's the kale, which is used in lots of Hawaiian dishes. I make this salad with orange segments as an appetizer, but you could substitute slices of smoked ham or grilled shrimp to make it lunch.

SERVES 8 AS AN APPETIZER OR SERVES 4 AS A MAIN COURSE

KALE

*1 large bunch kale (not baby kale),
  about ¾ pound, stemmed and sliced
  into ⅛-inch julienne*
½ teaspoon kosher salt or coarse sea salt
¼ teaspoon freshly ground black pepper
½ cup Miso-Sesame Vinaigrette

FOR ASSEMBLY

½ large sweet onion, sliced into ⅛-inch julienne
½ cup golden raisins
*½ cup roasted, salted macadamia nuts,
  coarsely chopped*
2 large oranges, divided into segments (optional)
Miso-Sesame Vinaigrette

PREPARE KALE

About 30 minutes to 1 hour before serving, place kale in a large bowl, season with salt and pepper and toss at least 12 times to bruise the leaves. Add miso vinaigrette and toss 12 more times.

ASSEMBLE

Just before serving, add onion, raisins and nuts, and toss well to combine. Add more vinaigrette to taste, or serve additional vinaigrette on the side. Garnish with orange segments, if desired.

Miso-Sesame Vinaigrette

INGREDIENTS

1 tablespoon white sesame seeds
½ tablespoon fennel seeds
½ cup canola oil
¼ cup rice wine vinegar
2 tablespoons white miso paste
1 tsp sriracha
½ teaspoon table salt
¼ teaspoon freshly ground black pepper
3 tablespoons honey
1 tablespoon molasses (light or dark)
1 tablespoon freshly squeezed lemon juice
2 small cloves garlic, minced (about 1 tablespoon)
½ small onion, chopped (about ¼ cup)

TOAST SEEDS

Heat oven to 350 degrees F. Place sesame seeds on a small baking sheet and toast in the oven for 2 minutes. Add fennel seeds and toast an additional 2 minutes. Transfer seeds to a clean bowl and let cool for 10 minutes. Using a spice grinder, mortar and pestle or food processor, grind seeds until pulverized and reserve.

PREPARE VINAIGRETTE

Place canola oil, vinegar, miso paste, sriracha, salt, pepper, honey, molasses, lemon juice, garlic and onion in a blender or food processor. Puree for 30 seconds to 1 minute. Pour into a bowl and stir in toasted seeds. Store vinaigrette in the refrigerator for up to 2 weeks. It will separate slightly; stir to remix.

Warm Pineapple Pepper Sauce

I created this sauce at home one Sunday afternoon to go with a spiral sliced ham. Pineapple is a traditional accompaniment, but I didn't want a sweet sauce. This one is savory with just a touch of sweetness—and yes, it really does call for a full teaspoon of ground pepper. The sauce also pairs well with pork chops and grilled swordfish.

MAKES 2 CUPS

SAUCE

*2 tablespoons plus 1 teaspoon
  unsalted butter, divided*
1 cup fresh pineapple, cut into ½ x ¼-inch batons
1 tablespoon dark brown sugar
*1 teaspoon freshly ground black pepper,
  large grind preferred*
½ cup sweet onion, diced
1 cup apple juice
*1 (1-inch) piece fresh ginger root,
  peeled and minced (about 1 tablespoon)*
¼ cup soy sauce or tamari sauce
2 tablespoons apple cider vinegar
2 tablespoons dark rum
*1 tablespoon cornstarch dissolved
  in 2 tablespoons cold water*

PREPARE PINEAPPLE

Heat a nonstick skillet over high heat for 1 to 2 minutes, until slightly smoking. Add 2 tablespoons of the butter. Add pineapple, distributing it in the pan, and then let sit, undisturbed, for 1 to 2 minutes until it begins to caramelize. Stir in sugar and black pepper. Transfer mixture to a clean bowl and set aside.

PREPARE SAUCE

Using the same skillet, reduce heat to medium, add onions and the additional teaspoon of butter. Sauté until onions are soft but not browned, 1 to 2 minutes. (They should turn a little brown from the brown sugar left in the pan, but do not allow them to caramelize.) Add apple juice, stir and bring to a simmer. Add ginger, soy sauce, vinegar and rum. Bring mixture to a boil. Stir cornstarch-water mixture and add to the boiling sauce. As soon as the sauce re-boils and thickens, which should be almost immediately, turn off heat and remove the skillet from the burner. Add pineapple mixture and stir well. Serve the sauce immediately or let cool and store for up to 48 hours; reheat the sauce before serving.

Dick Threlfall—Hawaiʻi
Island Goat Dairy

AFTER A COUPLE HOURS of touring and sipping coffee with friends on their coffee farm, we headed makai (toward the ocean). In less than a mile, we saw the Hawai'i Island Goat Dairy sign and impulsively turned in. It was mid-afternoon, and the owner, Dick Threlfall, was napping after delivering two kids the previous night. His brother-in-law woke him and we were soon tasting cheese.

The mainstay chèvre was as good as any. Dick, however, has a few special selections that are not on the market. We ended the day tasting the Crottin, fromage blanc and Valencay, which are out-of-this-world good. The entire time Dick regaled us with stories from his years of shoeing horses on the Big Island and "retiring" to the goat cheese farm.

Driving the old highway back to Waimea, with the ocean a few thousand feet below and Mauna Kea towering above, I could only think, *"Lucky live Hawai'i!"*

Panko-Crusted Goat Cheese Salad with Strawberry Vinaigrette

I created this salad to showcase the amazing strawberries from Kula, a town halfway up the western slope of Maui's Haleakala, and the goat cheese from small producers on the Big Island and Kaua'i. The recipe requires some planning ahead but is easy to assemble and very impressive in both appearance and flavor. I make it often when strawberries are in season.

SERVES 4 AS A SIDE SALAD OR SERVES 2 AS A LUNCHEON SALAD

CRUSTED GOAT CHEESE

1 (8-ounce) log fresh (not aged) goat cheese
¼ cup sweet onion, thinly sliced
8 ounces strawberries (about 16)
  hulled and quartered
¼ cup all-purpose flour
1 large egg, gently beaten
½ cup panko flakes
2 tablespoons vegetable oil

SALAD

4 ounces spring salad greens
  or other tender salad greens
1 recipe Strawberry Vinaigrette (page 90)

PREPARE GOAT CHEESE AND STRAWBERRIES

Slice goat cheese into 4 equal pieces and pat each slice into a 1½-inch-diameter round. Place rounds on a small baking sheet or plate, cover with plastic wrap and freeze for 10 minutes. In a small bowl, combine sliced onions and quartered strawberries; set aside.

Place 3 shallow bowls side by side: Place flour in one bowl, beaten egg in the second bowl, and panko flakes in the third bowl. Line a dinner plate with two layers of paper towel and place near the stove where you will fry the goat cheese.

Remove goat cheese rounds from the freezer; coat 1 round in flour, tapping off any excess; then submerge in the egg, letting any excess drip off; then coat in panko flakes and place on a clean plate. Repeat with remaining goat cheese rounds. In a cast iron or stainless steel skillet over medium heat, warm the oil for 30 seconds, or until shimmering. Carefully arrange coated goat cheese rounds in the skillet. Fry for 1 minute, turn, and fry for 1 minute more or until the cheese just barely begins to ooze. Remove to the paper towel-lined plate.

Recipe continued on page 90

Recipe continued from page 88

ASSEMBLE SALAD

In a large bowl, toss greens with ½ cup of the vinaigrette. Divide the dressed greens among salad plates. Add 2 tablespoons of the vinaigrette to reserved strawberries and onions, toss to combine and divide the strawberry mixture evenly among the plates, piling it next to the greens. Top each salad with 1 goat cheese round (2 each for luncheon salads). Drizzle salads with some of the remaining vinaigrette. Serve the remaining vinaigrette at the table.

Strawberry Vinaigrette

MAKES 1½ CUPS

INGREDIENTS

4 ounces strawberries (about 8) hulled and quartered

1 tablespoon granulated sugar

¼ teaspoon table salt

1 teaspoon chopped fresh parsley

1 teaspoon chopped fresh mint

1 shallot, chopped (about 2 teaspoons)

1 small clove garlic, finely chopped (about ½ teaspoon)

1 (¼-inch) piece fresh ginger root, peeled and quartered (about 1 scant teaspoon)

¼ cup cassis vinegar

½ cup vegetable oil

PREPARATION

In a blender or small food processor, combine strawberries, sugar, salt, parsley, mint, shallot, garlic, ginger and vinegar. Puree for 20 seconds, until herbs and vegetables are minced and integrated into the vinegar. With the blender or food processor running, gradually drizzle in oil until combined. The vinaigrette is best served fresh but can be refrigerated for up to 48 hours.

Merriman's Waimea

Maui Onion-Sesame Vinaigrette

Maui onions are famous for their sweetness, which many attribute to the volcanic soil they grow in and rain followed by bright sunshine. Other sweet onion varieties, like Walla Walla and Vidalia, are good substitutes.

MAKES 2 CUPS

INGREDIENTS

1 tablespoon olive oil

1 small sweet onion, quartered and thinly sliced

½ cup soy sauce or tamari

1 tablespoon red miso paste

1 tablespoon freshly squeezed lime juice

2 teaspoons rice wine vinegar

1 teaspoon dry mustard mixed
    with 1 teaspoon water

1 teaspoon toasted sesame oil

1 (1-inch) piece fresh ginger root,
    peeled and minced (about 1 tablespoon)

½ small clove garlic, minced (about 1 teaspoon)

2 tablespoons sambal oelek

½ cup canola oil

½ teaspoon salt

¼ teaspoon freshly ground black pepper

PREPARATION

Heat a skillet on medium-high heat for 1 minute. Add olive oil, swirling to coat the pan, and add onions. Cook, stirring constantly, for 5 to 8 minutes, until soft and golden. Transfer onions to a blender or food processor. Add soy sauce, miso paste, lime juice, vinegar, mustard, sesame oil, ginger, garlic and sambal oelek. Chop with 5 short pulses, then pulse continuously for 20 to 30 seconds to puree completely. With the blender or food processor running, slowly add the oil. Pour dressing into a bowl or jar, add salt and pepper and mix well.

Roasted Brussels Sprouts

The Brussels sprouts may be left whole or cut in half, depending on size. I usually leave the marble-sized sprouts whole, but slice the bigger ones in half for more even cooking. The outer leaves will get very brown and crispy, the perfect wrapping for these sweet and tender little cabbages.

SERVES 4 AS A SIDE DISH

INGREDIENTS

1 pound Brussels sprouts, trimmed and outer leaves removed
1 tablespoon olive oil
¼ teaspoon red pepper flakes
3–4 cloves garlic, thinly sliced
½ sweet onion, thinly sliced
½ red bell pepper, thinly sliced
1 (1-inch) piece fresh ginger root, peeled and thinly sliced, then julienned
1 teaspoon coarse sea salt or kosher salt
1 ounce Parmigiano-Reggiano cheese, thinly sliced (optional)

PREPARATION

Preheat the oven to 475 degrees F.

Place Brussels sprouts in a heavy-bottomed pan. Add olive oil and red pepper flakes, mix to coat the sprouts, then let sit while the oven preheats and you prepare the remaining ingredients.

Place the pan in the hot oven until the sprouts begin to brown, about 10 minutes. Add garlic and stir or shake the pan to redistribute. Continue roasting for about 5 minutes more, until the sprouts turn dark brown and begin to soften. Add onion, peppers, ginger and salt. Stir or shake the pan again and return to the oven for another 3 to 5 minutes. When sprouts are brown and fragrant, remove from the oven, add cheese (if using) and serve.

Smoked Taro Hummus

Taro (kalo in Hawaiian) is a starchy corm (root vegetable) that ranges in size from smaller than a tennis ball to bigger than a softball. If you cannot find taro in your local grocery, look for malanga. Or you might find dasheen (another name for malanga) in a Japanese grocery. Either of these makes a good substitute for taro. We serve this hummus with taro chips, fresh cucumber, raw radishes and whole romaine lettuce leaves. The crisp garden vegetables add a delightful contrast to the smoky flavor and thick texture of the taro puree.

Never eat raw taro! All taro contains calcium oxalate crystals, which can be irritating to the mouth and throat if the taro is not cooked thoroughly. Heat breaks down the crystals, and the cooked taro has a lovely soft consistency and tastes similar to a potato.

MAKES 3 TO 4 CUPS

TARO
1 pound taro root, peeled and cut into 2-inch chunks

HUMMUS
2 cups cooked or canned chickpeas,
    drained and rinsed

¼ cup tahini paste

¼ cup freshly squeezed lemon juice
    plus extra to taste

6 cloves garlic

1 teaspoon table salt, divided

½ teaspoon freshly ground black pepper, divided

¼ teaspoon liquid smoke

2 tablespoons canola oil

1 small onion, cut into ¼-inch dice (about ½ cup)

2 jalapeño peppers, cored,
    seeded and cut into ⅛-inch dice

PREPARE TARO
Place taro pieces in a large saucepan and add water to cover. Boil until soft, about 20 to 30 minutes, then drain in a colander and let cool for about 15 minutes.

PREPARE HUMMUS
While taro is cooling, place chickpeas, tahini, lemon juice, garlic, ½ teaspoon of the salt, ¼ teaspoon pepper and liquid smoke in a food processor. Process with 10 (2-second) pulses, then 2 (10-second) pulses, to puree mixture. Reserve in the food processor.

Heat canola oil in a sauté pan, add onions and jalapeño and cook on low to medium heat for about 4 minutes, or until soft. Add remaining ½ teaspoon salt and ¼ teaspoon pepper and stir well. Remove the pan from the heat.

Add cooked onions and jalapeño to the cooled taro and mash together. Add mixture to the food processor, and use 4 (15-second) pulses to puree all ingredients until smooth. Remove mixture to a bowl, cover tightly and let rest, refrigerated, for at least 30 minutes before serving. It will keep, if well covered, for several days. Just before serving, taste and add salt or lemon juice, as desired.

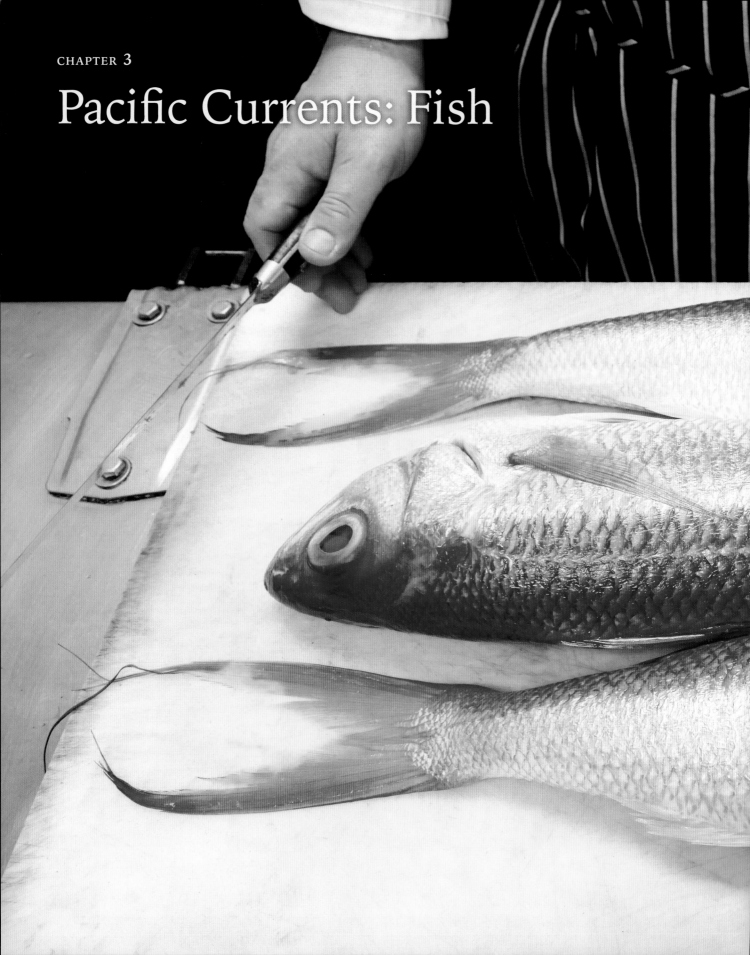

CHAPTER 3

Pacific Currents: Fish

Taking a Dive for the Food Network

IT ALL STARTED while I was working on recipes before opening The Gallery restaurant. In the middle of preparing a curry, I ran out of coconut milk, a key ingredient. The drive to the local market would have taken at least 30 minutes, so I just shinnied up a coconut palm out in the garden and hacked one off the tree. No big deal to me. I had also developed a creamy beurre blanc made with sea urchin roe from urchins I collected myself

from the ocean nearby and from the shallows and reefs at Paniau Beach—also not a big deal. Or so I thought. Apparently, I was earning a reputation among the locals as "the chef who would go to any length to get what he needed in the name of local cuisine."

When, a few years later, the Food Network called and asked if they could film me climbing a coconut palm and gathering sea urchins, I figured I could still make it up a tree and into a tide pool, so I said yes. The day before shooting, they added another stunt to the agenda: They wanted me to spear a fish! Although I'd done some spearfishing, I was no expert and I had visions of them filming for hours while

my spear remained empty. I asked a buddy, Harry Wishard, who was highly skilled with a spear, to help me out.

We met the film crew at Paniau. Harry had arrived earlier and already had some great-looking fish on his stringer. (He is part of a long tradition of free diving—no air tanks.) Harry lay motionless on the sea floor for a full 60 seconds as fish, no longer alarmed, returned. With imperceptible movement, he aimed the already cocked spear and let loose. Twenty feet away the spear pierced the head of its target. The underwater camera captured the shot, and the footage was spliced between me diving and then surfacing with a fish on my spear. Gotta love the visual media.

Later that afternoon, I climbed a Samoan coconut tree, a dwarf variety about 12 feet tall. If you saw the show, the reason I seem to be so high in the air is because the cameraman is lying on his back filming upwards. It's been years since that episode of *Extreme Cuisine* aired. I like to think I could still gather sea urchins, and maybe even some coconuts—from the ground under the palms—but spear a parrot fish? Only with a knife and fork.

Monkeypod's Coconut Fish Chowder

All three of my kids attended Seabury Hall, a prep school located high up on the slopes of Haleakala. Every spring the school held a fund-raising fair, and we participated with a Merriman's booth. Jessie, my youngest, says that the teachers would start pestering her right after the first of the year. "Is your dad coming to the fair—and is he going to make the fish chowder?" Now that my kids are out of school, I decided to add it to the Monkeypod Kitchen menu. Cooking the shrimp whole adds flavor to the chowder, but peeling and deveining them makes them easier to eat. Leaving just the tails on is a nice compromise. This soup base is also great with lobster, squash or tofu.

SERVES 6 AS AN APPETIZER OR SERVES 4 AS A MAIN COURSE

CHOWDER
1 cup clam juice

1 (½-inch) piece fresh galangal or fresh ginger
root, peeled and cut into ⅛-inch slices

2 stalks lemongrass, white stems cored
and finely chopped (about 2 tablespoons),
green tops kept whole

1 tablespoon nam pla or nuoc mam

1 teaspoon sriracha or sambal oelek

1 (13–14-ounce) can unsweetened coconut milk

12 jumbo shrimp (U-16/20),
peeled and deveined, with tails intact

12 sea scallops, abductor muscle removed

1 pound halibut or other mild, firm white fish,
skinned and cut into 2-inch squares

4 kaffir lime leaves (optional)

FOR ASSEMBLY
½ cup roasted, unsalted peanuts,
whole or large pieces

½ cup loosely packed fresh mint leaves
or fresh cilantro leaves, coarsely chopped

⅛ medium red onion, julienned

½ cup fresh bean sprouts

PREPARE CHOWDER

Place clam broth, galangal and lemongrass stems and tops in a large saucepan and bring to a boil over medium-high heat. Reduce heat and simmer 10 minutes. Add nam pla, sriracha and coconut milk. Stir to combine and simmer for 5 minutes more.

About 10 minutes before serving, bring broth to a boil and add the seafood. Return mixture to boiling. Roll lime leaves, if using, and add. *Kaffir lime leaves are not edible and should be removed before serving.* Cover, reduce heat as low as possible and simmer for 5 minutes.

ASSEMBLE

While the chowder cooks, toast peanuts in a dry skillet until just fragrant. Remove lemongrass tops and kaffir lime leaves. Ladle chowder into bowls and top each serving with a quarter of the mint, toasted peanuts, red onion and bean sprouts, or serve garnishes in separate dishes and allow diners to help themselves.

Merriman's Wok-Charred Ahi with Asian Slaw and Wasabi Dipping Sauce

Tataki is a traditional Japanese method for searing raw fish. This is our rendition of it. Back in 1986, we were probably one of the first restaurants in the US to serve seared ahi. I was not at all certain Americans would like it, but the dish was a huge hit and is still a favorite in all Merriman's restaurants. The ahi should be seared just before serving, so prepare the coating, slaw and dipping sauce ahead of time. When you're ready to serve, plate the slaw and divide the dipping sauce into bowls before cooking the ahi.

SERVES 8 AS AN APPETIZER OR SERVES 4 AS A MAIN COURSE

AHI COATING

2 shallots, minced (about ¹/₃ cup)
1 (2-inch) piece fresh ginger root, peeled and minced (about 2 tablespoons)
2 large cloves garlic, minced (about 1 tablespoon)
1 tablespoon fresh thyme leaves, whole
1 tablespoon plus 1 teaspoon dried marjoram
¹/₂ teaspoon red pepper flakes
1 teaspoon table salt
¹/₄ teaspoon freshly ground black pepper
¹/₄ teaspoon cayenne pepper
1 tablespoon plus 1 teaspoon freshly squeezed lemon juice
1¹/₂ cups clarified butter (page 116), melted and warm

PREPARE AHI COATING

Place shallots, ginger, garlic, thyme, marjoram, pepper flakes, salt, pepper, cayenne and lemon juice in a small bowl, and mix well. Add melted clarified butter and mix well. Chill coating for 30 minutes in the refrigerator, so that it thickens slightly, then stir to recombine ingredients. The coating can be chilled for up to 48 hours, during which time it will solidify. To use solidified coating, remove from the refrigerator 30 minutes before using, so it begins to melt at room temperature, and stir to recombine all ingredients.

ASIAN SLAW

¹/₂ head Napa cabbage, halved and sliced into ¹/₄-inch ribbons (about 2 cups)
²/₃ cup fresh bean sprouts
¹/₂ red onion, cut into ¹/₈-inch slices (about ²/₃ cup)
¹/₃ cup cilantro leaves, chopped

PREPARE ASIAN SLAW

Place cabbage, bean sprouts, onion and cilantro in a medium bowl and toss well. Chill until ready to serve. The slaw can be stored in the refrigerator for up to 48 hours.

Recipe continued on page 104

Recipe continued from page 103

WASABI DIPPING SAUCE

2 tablespoons wasabi powder

2 tablespoons water

1 cup soy sauce

$^1/_3$ cup freshly squeezed lemon juice

$^1/_3$ cup mirin

PREPARE WASABI DIPPING SAUCE

In a small bowl, mix wasabi and water to make a thick paste. Add soy sauce, lemon juice and mirin. Whisk to combine, making sure the wasabi is completely dissolved into the liquid. The sauce can be stored in the refrigerator for up to 48 hours. To serve, bring to room temperature and divide among individual bowls.

WOK-CHARRED AHI

Ahi Coating, room temperature

4 (6-ounce) sashimi-grade pieces ahi tuna,
    (block-like pieces that are 1½–2 inches thick by 5 inches long work best)

PREPARE AHI

Heat a skillet or wok on high heat until very hot. Spread a thin layer of the coating on 3 pieces of the ahi, making sure to create a crust of shallot, garlic and ginger. Place coated ahi pieces in the skillet with at least 1 inch between each piece, and sear for 30 seconds on each side. Transfer seared tuna to a cutting board. Repeat the coating and cooking process with remaining 'ahi and transfer to the cutting board.

ASSEMBLE

Slice seared ahi, across the grain, into ¼-inch slices. Place Asian Slaw onto a serving platter or divide among individual plates, and arrange overlapping ahi slices alongside the slaw. Serve with Wasabi Dipping Sauce.

Merriman's Fish House, Poipu, Kaua'i

"Do The Right Thing"

Sautéed Snapper with Miso Beurre Blanc

We like to serve opakapaka or onaga (both are types of snapper) at Merriman's. You can use any type of snapper or substitute with rockfish, grouper, cod, sole or any other moist white fish. The sauce is a variation on a classic French beurre blanc with an extra boost of umami from the miso paste.

SERVES 4

FISH

*4 (6–7-ounce) opakapaka filets,
    skinless and boneless*

Kosher salt

Freshly ground black pepper

1 tablespoon vegetable oil

*½ shallot, halved lengthwise
    and sliced ¹⁄₁₆-inch thick (about 1 tablespoon)*

¾ cup dry white wine

BEURRE BLANC

*6 tablespoons unsalted butter, lightly chilled
    and cut into matchbook-size pieces*

*1 tablespoon red miso paste,
    dissolved in 1 tablespoon water*

2 teaspoons mirin

Pinch of cayenne pepper

Pinch of kosher salt

PREPARE FISH

Preheat the oven to 500 degrees F.

Season bone side of the fish with salt and pepper. Heat an oven-proof sauté pan over medium-high heat for about 3 minutes. Add oil and heat for about 1 minute. (The oil should have the consistency of water, but should not smoke.) Place fish in the pan, seasoned side down. Cook for 2 minutes, or until the edges turn white. (Do not stir the fish while cooking.) Add sliced shallots to the pan, and cook 1 minute, stirring occasionally but avoiding the fish. Turn fish carefully and add white wine. Place the pan, uncovered, in the oven and cook about 7 minutes for 1½-inch-thick opakapaka, and maybe 2 minutes for a skinny little rockfish. When filets feel firm, remove from the oven and immediately transfer fish to a platter.

PREPARE BEURRE BLANC

Return the pan with the remaining liquid to the stovetop on medium-high heat. Bring to a boil, and continue cooking until it has reduced by about half. Reduce the heat to medium. Whisk in 1 to 3 pieces of the butter at a time, stirring constantly, and being sure each addition of butter is completely incorporated before adding more. (This ensures the sauce remains at an even temperature. If it gets too cold or too hot, it will curdle.) When all the butter is completely incorporated, turn off the heat and stir in miso, mirin, cayenne pepper and salt. Taste and adjust the seasonings, as needed. Spoon sauce over each filet and serve immediately.

Tips for Cooking Fish

- The most important variable in cooking fish is the thickness of the filet. It is much more important than the cooking method.
- For grilling, pan-frying or baking, the best estimate for total cooking time is 10 minutes per 1 inch of thickness.
- Remember that the fish will continue cooking, if it's kept warm, after it's removed from the grill, pan or oven.
- The exception is microwave cooking, so I am including my secret for cooking fish in a microwave.
- When sautéing, cook the fish bone side first.
- When plating, serve the cooked-first side up as that side will have the best appearance.
- Preheating the pan or grill helps prevent the fish from sticking.
- Continuation cooking means the fish will continue to cook a bit more after it is plated. Remove fish from the heat a little early to avoid overcooking.

MICROWAVE-COOKED FISH

Start with thick filets (1 inch or thicker). Rub with vegetable or peanut oil, season with salt and pepper. Heat a heavy skillet over high heat for 1 to 2 minutes. Add the filets and cook just until seared on both sides, about 1 minute per side. Remove the filets to a microwave-safe plate and let them cool while you make a simple sauce. When the filets are cooled, wrap them airtight in plastic wrap.

Simple sauce: Using the same skillet, sauté chopped shallots, deglaze with white wine or lemon juice, add a few capers, then a few pats of cold butter, one at a time.

When you unwrap the fish, don't forget to add the juices to your sauce! When it's time to serve, reheat the sauce in the microwave. Then microwave the fish. How long depends on the microwave and the thickness of the filets. Start with 1 minute on high, then check the fish. When it flakes easily with a fork, or feels firm to the touch, it is done. If needed, continue cooking in 15- to 30-second increments. (If you're cooking 1½-inch-thick ono filets, and using the microwave in my kitchen, count on 1 minute 40 seconds on high.)

Hula Grill's Screamin' Sesame Opah with Tangy Ponzu Sauce

Yanagi Sushi is one of those great little sushi bars in Honolulu. Yanagi glazes their scallops with a delicious soy-mayonnaise topping. I decided to combine that concept with the flavors of spicy sesame dishes you often find in Hawai'i. Try it with cold sake. You'll thank me.

SERVES 4

FISH

4 (6-ounce) opah or mahi-mahi filets, skinless
4 tablespoons sesame seeds, divided
1 small clove garlic, chopped (about ¹/₂ teaspoon)
1 (1-inch) piece fresh ginger root,
  peeled and finely chopped (about 1 tablespoon)
1 cup mayonnaise
1 teaspoon toasted sesame oil

FOR ASSEMBLY

2 cups cooked white or brown rice
Tangy Ponzu Sauce
4 scallions, green parts only, cut into
  ¹/₄-inch lengths

PREPARE FISH

Preheat the oven to 450 degrees F.

Place fish filets on a baking sheet or in a shallow baking pan. In a small bowl, stir together 2 tablespoons of the sesame seeds, garlic, ginger, mayonnaise and oil. Spread mixture evenly among the filets. Sprinkle remaining sesame seeds evenly over the mayonnaise coating. Bake 10 to 12 minutes, or until the topping is golden brown and the fish can be flaked with a fork.

ASSEMBLY

Divide rice evenly among 4 plates and top with a fish filet. Spoon 3 tablespoons of the sauce over each filet and garnish with scallions.

Tangy Ponzu Sauce

This sauce can be made a day ahead and refrigerated; leftover sauce can be used with other fish, chicken or vegetables.

MAKES ABOUT 1¹/₄ CUPS

SAUCE

¹/₂ cup soy sauce
¹/₂ cup water
1 tablespoon rice wine vinegar
¹/₄ teaspoon red pepper flakes
1 (¹/₂-inch) piece fresh ginger root, peeled and finely chopped
  (about ¹/₂ tablespoon)
¹/₂ teaspoon dark-roasted sesame oil
2 tablespoons freshly squeezed lemon juice

PREPARE SAUCE

In a bowl, whisk together all ingredients. Pass extra sauce at the table.

Onaga with Charred Tomato and Fennel

I never got into the sun-dried tomato craze, but I have always loved a baked or roasted tomato. This recipe goes one step further and puts a nice char on both the tomatoes and the fennel, deepening the flavor without overpowering the fish. My brother was skeptical about the splash of tequila at the end—until he tasted the dish both with and without it. His comment? "Wow! The tequila really brings out all the other flavors." I agree.

SERVES 4

INGREDIENTS

1 bulb fennel, quartered and cored
2 tomatoes, halved at the equator and cored
4 (5-ounce) onaga or other snapper filets, with or without skin
1 teaspoon salt
¼ teaspoon freshly ground black pepper
2 tablespoons olive oil
¼ cup onion, chopped

FOR ASSEMBLY

Zest and juice of 1 lime
3 tablespoons good-quality tequila (I use Jose Cuervo silver)

PREPARE TOMATO AND FENNEL

Preheat the oven to broil, on high setting, if available.

Cut each fennel quarter into ¼-inch slices. Place tomatoes, cut side down, into an ovenproof skillet or pan and place under the broiler until tomato skin turns black, about 2 to 3 minutes depending on the broiler temperature. Turn tomatoes over and broil another 2 to 3 minutes. Add sliced fennel and broil for 2 more minutes. Remove tomato and fennel to a cutting board and let cool slightly. Remove skin from tomatoes and chop into ½-inch pieces, keeping them separate from fennel.

PREPARE FISH

If using unskinned fish, make 3 parallel cuts, just through the skin, on each filet. Season both sides of fish with salt and pepper. Heat a skillet on high heat for 1 minute. Add olive oil to the skillet, then add fish filets, skin (or skinned) side down. Cook 4 minutes; turn filets and cook 4 minutes more. (See Tips for Cooking Fish, pages 106-107, and adjust time to about 10 minutes total per 1-inch thickness.) Remove fish to a plate.

ASSEMBLE

Adjust heat to medium-high, and add onions and tomatoes to the skillet. Cook for 2 minutes, add fennel and cook 1 more minute. Turn off heat and stir in lime zest and juice. Spoon vegetables onto a platter or individual plates and splash with tequila. Place fish on top and serve.

Macadamia Nut–Crusted Ono

At Merriman's, Monkeypod Kitchen by Merriman and Hula Grill Ka'anapali, macadamia-crusted is our most popular fish preparation. Ono is a Hawaiian word meaning delicious, and fresh ono is all that. Ono is known as wahoo in other parts of the country. If you cannot get wahoo, use any firm white fish, like halibut or king mackerel, that will stand up to the macadamia nut crust. I like to serve this dish with Spicy Greens with Grilled Pineapple (page 60) and, of course, some white rice.

SERVES 6

MAC NUT CRUST

1 cup roasted, unsalted macadamia nuts
or use salted nuts and reduce the kosher salt
to ½ teaspoon
¼ cup panko flakes
1½ teaspoons garlic powder
Zest of 2 lemons (about 1 tablespoon)
½ teaspoon cayenne pepper
1½ teaspoons kosher salt
2 tablespoons chopped fresh flat-leaf parsley
1½ teaspoons Worcestershire sauce
2 tablespoons butter, melted

PREPARE CRUST

Place macadamia nuts, panko flakes, garlic powder, lemon zest, cayenne pepper, salt and parsley in a food processor and chop with 5 to 10 (3-second) pulses, until nuts are uniform in size but still chunky. Transfer mixture to a bowl. Add Worcestershire sauce and melted butter. Mix with a fork to combine. Set aside.

FISH

1 tablespoon table salt
¾ teaspoon freshly ground black pepper
6 (6-ounce) ono filets, skinless
6 tablespoons mayonnaise
Mac Nut Crust
2 tablespoons chopped fresh flat-leaf parsley

PREPARE FISH

Preheat the oven to 450 degrees F.

Mix together salt and pepper. Place fish in a glass baking dish. Spread 1 tablespoon of the mayonnaise on each filet, and follow with ½ teaspoon of the salt and pepper mixture. Spoon about ¼ cup of the crust mixture over each filet, pressing into the mayonnaise. Bake fish for 12 minutes. Remove from the oven and place fish on a serving platter. Sprinkle with parsley.

A Note about Cooking Time: Ono filets are about 1 inch thick. If using a different kind of fish, or thicker filets (I don't recommend thinner ones), you may need to increase the cooking time. Use an instant-read thermometer to ensure the interior of the fish reaches 140 degrees F, and reduce the oven temperature if the crust is getting too brown. Or, if the fish is done but the crust is not brown, place under the broiler for 1 to 2 minutes, watching carefully to avoid burning.

Fish Tacos—Moku's Way

Okay, there must be 50 ways to make fish tacos (apologies to Paul Simon). I did it my way (shout-out to Frank Sinatra) and used marinated fish, instead of fried. I most often use firm white fish like mahi-mahi or halibut. At home, I like to lay out a taco bar with lots of fixings, like Roasted Poblano Sour Cream (page 52), Pineapple Cole Slaw (page 69), Tomato-Mango Salsa (page 118) and some roughly chopped cilantro or parsley, and let folks build their own. Fair warning—these puppies are messy, but, oh, so good—I recommend taco holders, which can be purchased from kitchen suppliers.

FISH

1½ pounds mahi-mahi or halibut, skinless and boneless
2 tablespoons clarified butter (page 116)

MARINADE

1 tablespoon coriander seeds
4 large cloves garlic, roughly chopped
1 tablespoon ground cumin
½ tablespoon red pepper flakes
2 teaspoons smoked paprika
2 teaspoons kosher salt
¾ cup canola oil
3 tablespoons extra-virgin olive oil
3 tablespoons freshly squeezed lemon juice
1 tablespoon fresh cilantro leaves

MARINATE FISH

Cut fish into 12 logs, slicing across the filet. Place fish logs into a resealable plastic bag.

Toast coriander seeds in a dry skillet until just fragrant. Watch carefully to avoid burning. Allow seeds to cool, then grind with a mortar and pestle or in a spice grinder. Place ground seeds into a blender or food processor and add garlic, cumin, red pepper flakes, paprika, salt, canola oil, olive oil, lemon juice and cilantro leaves. Process with 3 (2-second) pulses to combine, then pulse continuously for 5 to 10 seconds. Pour marinade over fish, securely seal the bag and gently turn to distribute the marinade and coat each piece well. Let sit at room temperature for 30 minutes, or in the refrigerator for up to 2 hours. Remove fish just before cooking and place in a colander to drain excess marinade.

TOMATILLO SALSA

1 pound tomatillos (about 10)
1 large sweet onion, chopped
1 medium clove garlic, minced (about 1 teaspoon)
1½ cups water mixed with 1 tablespoon kosher salt
3 tablespoons fresh cilantro leaves, divided
¼ cup freshly squeezed lime juice, divided
1 teaspoon kosher salt, divided
½ teaspoon freshly ground black pepper, divided
Pinch of cayenne pepper

Recipe continued on page 116

Recipe continued from page 115

GARNISHES

¼ head white cabbage, julienned

1 small avocado

2 small tomatoes or 1 large tomato

FOR ASSEMBLY

2 tablespoons clarified butter (page 116)

12 (6-inch) corn tortillas

PREPARE SALSA AND GARNISHES

Cut each tomatillo in half at the equator, then slice each half into quarters. Place half of the tomatillos in a 1-quart saucepan and add onion and garlic. Add salted water and stir. Bring mixture to a boil, then reduce to a simmer and cook for 2 minutes. Remove from the heat and strain tomatillo mixture. Let mixture cool at room temperature.

Place uncooked tomatillos into a blender or food processor. Add 1 tablespoon of the cilantro leaves, 2 tablespoons of the lime juice, ½ teaspoon of the salt, ¼ teaspoon of the black pepper and the cayenne pepper. Blend or process with 2 (3-second) pulses to mix, and then 2 (5-second) pulses to puree. Pour mixture into a bowl, and let cool. When cooked tomatillo mixture is cool, stir into the raw mixture.

Place cabbage in a small bowl and add remaining lime juice, salt and black pepper. Toss to combine.

Peel avocado, remove pit, and cut into a ½-inch dice. Cut tomatoes into a ½-inch dice.

PREPARE FISH

Prepare sauces and garnishes as directed. Cook fish in a cast iron skillet or on a griddle. Heat the pan or griddle for 5 minutes on medium-high heat. Add 1 tablespoon butter, and when melted add 4 to 6 fish logs, being careful not to crowd them. Cook for 2 minutes, turn, and cook 2 to 3 minutes more, until just flaking. Transfer cooked fish to a dish and cover loosely with aluminum foil. Repeat with the remaining fish logs.

ASSEMBLE

Warm each tortilla in a dry skillet, turning once. Compose each taco by layering 1 fish log, a portion of the dressed cabbage, 1 tablespoon of the tomatillo salsa, a few chunks of the avocado, a few chunks of the tomato, and some cilantro leaves. Roll or fold the taco and place in a taco holder, if you have them. Serve with lots of napkins!

Clarified Butter

Because clarified butter has a higher smoke point than regular butter, you can use it to pan-fry meat or fish at a higher temperature. If half a pound seems like a lot of butter, don't worry, about a quarter of it will be lost in the cooking process.

MAKES 1½ CUPS

INGREDIENTS

½ pound unsalted butter, cut into pieces

Cheesecloth

PREPARATION

Place butter in a heavy saucepan over very low heat. Slowly melt, watching carefully so butter does not brown or burn. When completely melted, remove from the heat and let stand for 5 minutes. Place 3 to 4 layers of cheesecloth into a strainer and position over a container with a tight-fitting lid. Skim foam from the top of the melted butter, then slowly pour butter through the cheesecloth layers into the container. Seal container tightly and store in the refrigerator for up to 1 month.

From left to right:
Chef Zac Sato, Uku, Asa Suguitan, Ono

Opakapaka with Spicy Liliko'i Sauce and Tomato-Mango Salsa

This has always been one of Merriman's most popular fish dishes. Opakapaka is Hawaiian pink snapper. The filets are fairly thin so they cook quickly. I love how the sweet liliko'i (passion fruit) sauce plays against the tangy lime and the spiciness of the salsa. We serve this particular fish with a mixture of white and black rice, or sweet potato palau.

SERVES 6

TOMATO-MANGO SALSA
12 cherry tomatoes
½ mango, peeled and cut into ½-inch dice
¼ seedless cucumber,
    peeled and cut into ¼-inch dice
4 scallions, white and green parts, thinly sliced
½ cup loosely packed fresh cilantro leaves, minced
¼ jalapeño pepper, seeded and minced
¼ cup freshly squeezed lime juice
2 tablespoons olive oil
½ teaspoon table salt
¼ teaspoon freshly ground black pepper

LILIKO'I SAUCE
1 cup chicken stock or vegetable stock
½ cup liliko'i puree or concentrate (often frozen)
1 tablespoon sugar
1 teaspoon sambal oelek
1 (½-inch) piece fresh ginger root, peeled and
    sliced into thin sticks
1 small shallot, diced
1½ teaspoons nam pla
1½ teaspoons cornstarch
2 tablespoons water
2 tablespoons unsalted butter,
    cold and cut into 2 pieces

FISH
6 (6-ounce) opakapaka filets, skinless
6 tablespoons canola oil, divided
Kosher salt
Freshly ground black pepper
½ cup sesame seeds, lightly toasted in a dry skillet

PREPARE SALSA
Cut each cherry tomato in half and place in a bowl. Add mango, cucumber, scallions, cilantro, jalapeño pepper, lime juice, olive oil, salt and pepper. Toss thoroughly. The salsa can be prepared up to 8 hours prior to serving and stored in the refrigerator.

START LILIKO'I SAUCE
Place chicken stock in a small saucepan over medium heat. Add liliko'i puree, sugar, sambal oelek, ginger, shallot and nam pla. Bring to a boil, then lower the heat and simmer 10 minutes, stirring every 2 to 3 minutes. Dissolve cornstarch in water and whisk into sauce. Continue to simmer sauce for 5 minutes, then remove from the heat. Prior to adding the butter, the sauce can be held in the saucepan for up to 1 hour, or stored up to 12 hours in the refrigerator.

PREPARE FISH

Preheat the oven to 350 degrees F.

On the bone side (nonskin side) of each filet, rub ½ tablespoon of the oil and sprinkle with a pinch of salt and pepper. Press toasted sesame seeds onto the other side of each filet. Heat a heavy-bottomed skillet over high heat for 2 to 3 minutes, until smoking hot, then add remaining 3 tablespoons oil. (Use 2 skillets, if necessary, splitting the oil between them, to avoid crowding the fish when added.) Place fish in the skillet, oil side down, and cook for 3 to 5 minutes, until filets can be easily lifted from the pan with a spatula. Turn fish once and cook 1 minute more. Remove fish and place on an ovensafe dish; avoid overlapping the filets. Place the dish in the hot oven, then turn the oven off.

FINISH LILIKO'I SAUCE

Add sauce to the skillet (if using 2 skillets, add sauce to only 1 of them), and bring to a boil. Add cold butter, whisking until it is melted into the sauce.

ASSEMBLE

Remove fish from the oven. Place 1 filet on each serving plate, and spoon some sauce over each. Garnish plates with salsa. Pass additional sauce at the table.

Merriman's Fish House,
Poipu, Kaua'i

Ahi Katsu with Lemon Sauce

Katsu is breaded fried meat, usually pork, and is very popular in Japan and Hawaiʻi. I like the crunch of Japanese panko flakes and thought they would be perfect for breading ahi steaks. Lemon sauce is not traditional with katsu—except for me, as it reminds me of the schnitzel served with lemon wedges we made in Germany. This sauce is simple to make and gets its deep, complex flavor from the way the nuttiness of the brown butter blends with the capers and lemon.

SERVES 4

AHI KATSU
4 (4–5-ounce) ahi steaks, 1¼–1½ inches thick
1½ cups panko breadcrumbs
¼ cup vegetable oil
2 teaspoons salt
½ teaspoon freshly ground black pepper

LEMON SAUCE
8 tablespoons unsalted butter, divided into 8 pieces
2 heaping tablespoons chopped fresh
    flat-leaf parsley
½ cup capers, drained well
2 tablespoons freshly squeezed lemon juice
Lemon supremes, cut from 1 lemon (optional)

PREPARE AHI
Pat ahi steaks dry with paper towels. Spread panko evenly on a flat pan or plate, and press ahi firmly into panko to coat both sides. Preheat a large sauté pan over high heat for 1 minute. Add oil to the very hot pan, swirling gently to coat. Add ahi, cooking about 2 minutes per side for rare tuna. (If cooking longer, you may need to lower the heat slightly to avoid burning the panko.) Remove ahi to a platter and season each side liberally with salt and a touch of the pepper. Sprinkle tops with a pinch of the parsley chopped for the sauce.

PREPARE LEMON SAUCE
Discard three-quarters of the oil remaining in the sauté pan and return to the stovetop over high heat. Add 6 tablespoons of the butter (carefully, as it will foam up). Cook, stirring constantly, until butter is brown and most of the foam has subsided. Add remaining parsley and fry for 5 seconds. Add capers and cook 30 seconds more. Turn off the heat. Add lemon juice and stir in remaining 2 tablespoons butter. Add lemon supremes, if using, and allow to partially melt into the sauce.

ASSEMBLE
Place 1 piece of ahi on each of 4 serving plates. Spoon sauce over fish.

Ponzu-Marinated Mahi-Mahi

My apologies to Japanese chefs, as my ponzu is not authentic. This has been one of Merriman's most requested dishes over the years. I like to serve this with rice and julienned vegetables, such as shiitake mushrooms, carrots, sweet onions and red bell peppers, sautéed in olive oil with fresh minced garlic, salt and pepper, and drizzled with a little of the reserved ponzu marinade.

SERVES 6

FISH
Ponzu Marinade
6 (6-ounce) mahi-mahi filets, skinned
¼ cup cornstarch
2–3 tablespoons vegetable oil

MARINATE FISH
Place mahi-mahi filets in a shallow dish. Pour the remaining marinade over the fish to cover. Marinate, at room temperature, for 15 to 20 minutes.

PONZU MARINADE
1 cup rice wine vinegar
3 tablespoons frozen orange juice concentrate
½ cup soy sauce
2 tablespoon dried ground ginger
½ cup granulated sugar
2 tablespoons freshly squeezed lemon juice
2 large cloves garlic, minced (about 1 tablespoon)
6 scallions, white and green parts,
    minced (about ¼ cup)
½ teaspoon sriracha

PREPARE MARINADE
Place all ingredients in a medium bowl and whisk to combine until the sugar is dissolved. Reserve ½ cup of marinade for serving the fish.

COOK FISH
Remove filets from marinade and shake gently to remove excess. Dredge filets in cornstarch.

Heat oil in a skillet over medium-high heat until it shimmers. Lower heat to medium, add filets, and cook 4 to 5 minutes per side, until nicely browned and the flesh flakes easily with a fork. Remove cooked filets to a paper towel-lined plate.

Drizzle with reserved marinade and serve, or use it to deglaze the skillet for a warm sauce.

Firecracker Fish Soup from Hula Grill Ka'anapali

Everybody knows somebody who claims to like really spicy food. This soup is for those people. Of course, you can turn the heat up or down by adjusting the number of jalapeño peppers (use the ribs and seeds for even more heat) and the amount of red pepper flakes or chipotle peppers. The soup is fairly thick, like a warm gazpacho. The cool (by comparison) corn mixture is the perfect foil to the firecracker-hot soup. In the restaurant, we serve some of the shrimp whole, but at home, I always peel and chop them before cooking.

SERVES 8 AS AN APPETIZER OR SERVES 4 AS A MAIN COURSE

SPICY SOUP

1 tablespoon canola oil

2 red bell peppers, diced

2 onions, diced

5 cloves garlic, chopped

1 jalapeño pepper, seeds and ribs removed, minced

1 stalk celery, sliced

½ teaspoon red pepper flakes

½ teaspoon dried oregano

½ teaspoon fennel seeds

½ teaspoon ground cumin

¼ teaspoon ground coriander

2 cups (16 ounces) canned Italian plum tomatoes, with juice

2 cups chicken stock

1 teaspoon canned chipotle peppers with adobo sauce

1 teaspoon salt

6 corn tortillas, toasted and torn into 2-inch pieces

CORN AND SEAFOOD

2 tablespoons canola oil, divided

3 cups corn kernels, freshly cut from cob or thawed from frozen

8 colossal shrimp (U-15), peeled, deveined, and chopped

8 ounces snapper filet, skinned and diced

2 tablespoons chopped cilantro

2 tablespoons extra-virgin olive oil

2 tablespoons freshly squeezed lime juice

½ teaspoon salt

PREPARE SPICY SOUP

Place canola oil in a large saucepan over medium-high heat. Add bell peppers, onion, garlic, jalapeño, celery, red pepper flakes, oregano, fennel seeds, cumin and coriander. Stir to coat vegetables with spices and oil. When vegetables begin to sizzle, turn heat to medium-low, cover and cook until soft but not brown, about 7 minutes. Add toma-

Recipe continued on page 128

Recipe continued from page 127
toes, stock, chipotle pepper and salt. Stir to combine, cover and simmer for 20 minutes. Add toasted tortillas, stir and cook 3 minutes more. Carefully add soup to a blender or food processor and puree. Return soup to the saucepan and keep warm over low heat.

PREPARE CORN AND SEAFOOD

Heat a large sauté pan on high for 30 seconds. Add 1 tablespoon of the canola oil and sauté corn kernels until they begin to brown. Transfer to a bowl. On high heat add ½ tablespoon of the canola oil and sauté shrimp, cooking 1 to 2 minutes, until pink. Add shrimp to reserved corn. Using the remaining ½ teaspoon canola oil, sauté snapper for 1 to 2 minutes, depending on thickness, until fish begins to fall apart, and add to corn and shrimp. Add cilantro, olive oil, lime juice and remaining ½ teaspoon salt. Mix gently but thoroughly.

ASSEMBLE

To serve, ladle soup into bowls and garnish with corn and seafood mixture.

Chef Sandy Barr

IN OUR KITCHENS we use the title "Chef" in its classical form. Only one person in the kitchen is the chief, or chef. The rest of us are proud to call ourselves cooks. Once I started opening more restaurants, it became impossible for me to function as chef in any of my kitchens. After me, Sandy Barr was the first person to hold the title at Merriman's Waimea.

Sandy and I met at the Mauna Lani when I was the hotel's banquet chef. Sandy joined me as the only full-time banquet cook, and we developed a great rapport. When I made the leap to The Gallery restaurant, Sandy signed on as cook and together we took those first steps toward defining Hawai'i Regional Cuisine. When Vicki and I opened Merriman's, I was lucky that Sandy agreed to cook by my side and cover my back.

In the 17 years she spent in the kitchen with me, Sandy did as much to define Merriman's cuisine as anyone—like the recipe for Ponzu-Marinated Mahi-Mahi. She brought that exciting combination of intellect and passion to her cooking—and she simply loved being at the stove. For Sandy, cooking is art, but not that pretentious "look at me" kind of art. For her, cooking is about turning out a perfectly seasoned, great-tasting dish, rather than displaying her extraordinary creativity. It's hard, if not impossible, to find a better cook than Sandy.

A few years ago Sandy left Merriman's to teach culinary arts at the local college. I just hope her students realize how fortunate they are to learn from one of the best.

Grilled Ahi with Coconut Curry

Growing up in Pittsburgh, coconut was a sweet suitable only for desserts. But in Hawai'i, most every luau features some sort of savory coconut with fish or chicken. I worked out this recipe soon after opening Merriman's in Waimea. Barbara Fairchild, former editor-in-chief of *Bon Appetit* magazine, came in the first night we served it as a special and she loved it, so we put it on the menu. A good fish market will grade its yellowfin tuna (ahi's English name), and this recipe works best with medium-grade fish—no sense wasting money on sashimi-quality tuna if you're cooking it. At Merriman's, we like ahi steaks that are 1 to 2 inches thick.

SERVES 6

SAUCE

1 teaspoon Madras curry powder

2 stalks lemongrass, leaves and core removed, finely chopped

2 tablespoons freshly grated ginger root

½ cup bottled clam juice

1 cup coconut milk (Sorry Bond, not stirred nor shaken. With as little jostling as possible, open the can at the end that's been upright in the pantry so the thick cream floats on top; then measure out 1 cup using all the cream and just enough of the liquid to make 1 cup.)

2 teaspoons nam pla

4 kaffir lime leaves (optional)

FISH

6 (6–7-ounce) ahi steaks, skinless

2 tablespoons vegetable oil or olive oil

1½ teaspoons salt

¾ teaspoon freshly ground black pepper

PREPARE GRILL

If using a gas grill, preheat on high with the lid down for 20 minutes. If using charcoal, light the grill 30 to 45 minutes before cooking; once the flames are gone, test it periodically. It's ready when you can't hold the back of your hand over the heat for 5 seconds.

PREPARE SAUCE

While the grill is heating, place curry powder in a dry stainless steel or nonstick saucepan (not aluminum or copper) and sauté over medium heat for 1 minute, stirring constantly. The curry will become fragrant as it heats, but watch carefully so it does not burn. Add lemongrass, ginger and clam juice and simmer, uncovered, for 10 minutes. Stir in coconut milk and simmer 5 minutes more. Remove sauce from the heat. If using lime leaves, roll or fold to release their flavor and add. Stir in nam pla. Keep sauce warm over the lowest possible heat until the fish is ready. *Kaffir lime leaves are not edible. Remove leaves before serving.*

GRILL FISH

Brush one side of ahi steaks with oil and season each with ¼ teaspoon salt and ⅛ teaspoon pepper. Place on the grill, oiled side down, and cook until the lighter color creeps a quarter of the way up the fish, about 7 minutes. Turn fish and cook for about 3 more minutes. Transfer to a platter or individual serving plates and spoon a generous portion of sauce down the middle, leaving some of the fish exposed.

CHAPTER 4

Big Island Lamb and Beef

Monty Richards—Snout to Tail for 25 Years

SMART, TOUGH, FUN and self-deprecating—qualities that come to mind when I think about Hawai'i rancher Monty Richards. For more than 80 years, the Kahua Ranch has been raising livestock on the slopes of Kohala mountain at the northern end of the Big Island. As Kahua's owner, Monty is determined to keep ranching a viable part of the Hawai'i lifestyle. He feels a strong responsibility to the paniolo (Hawaiian cowboys) and their families who have lived and worked the ranch for generations.

My first interaction with Monty was a 1984 phone call.

"Peter," he said, after introducing himself, "I'd like you to consider using our frozen Kahua lamb for your next imu." (An imu is an earthen oven typically used for roasting pigs, usually for luaus.)

As the brash and overly confident 20-something chef, I told the venerable rancher "We don't do luaus, and we only use fresh meat in the restaurant."

Monty's response was simple. "You want fresh lamb, you gotta buy the whole animal."

My brash, overly confident reply? "Okay, sounds good." Thus began a more-than-20-year tradition of featuring a different cut of lamb every night at Merriman's.

Monty's fresh, whole lambs have helped define what makes Merriman's unique—highly skilled cooks using often-forgotten techniques, combined with a contemporary perspective and philosophy of sustainability. Training a broiler cook to grill perfect lamb chops every night is challenging enough, but employing professionals capable of handling a different part of the animal each day is just a completely different enterprise. Using the entire lamb, not only the preferred cuts, forces us to rely on age-old cooking techniques honed over time. We now do this with grass-fed beef from several Hawai'i ranches, as well as with wild boar from the macadamia nut fields in Ka'u, at the southern tip of the Big Island.

On Maui, we serve Maui Cattle Company beef and Malama Farms pasture-raised pork. On Kaua'i, Makaweli beef, Omao Ranch lamb and Kaneshiro pork make the menu. On O'ahu, our Monkeypod and Moku chefs use Shinsato Farm pork and Big Island beef. Kahua Ranch lamb is still a signature item on our menu, and like so many of the dishes we helped pioneer, we sort of stumbled onto it. We had no way of foreseeing that 20 years on, our diners would still clamor for a snout-to-tail experience, and we certainly never thought of ourselves then as locavores. We just knew we wanted to offer the experience of eating great-tasting, totally fresh food raised right here on the island.

Thanks Monty.

Lamb Chops with Cabernet and Papaya

Lamb paired with red wine is a classic combination. When you add some papaya it becomes classic Hawai'i. Of course we use the local lamb. If I am cooking on the mainland, I always look for Colorado lamb because I think it tastes best. By all means, use whatever good-quality lamb you can find. With the butter, wine, spices and papaya, it's all good.

SERVES 4 AS AN APPETIZER OR SERVES 2 AS A MAIN COURSE

LAMB CHOPS AND PAPAYA

8 lamb rib chops
1 teaspoon coriander seeds
2 tablespoons Dijon mustard
2 tablespoons freshly squeezed lemon juice
2 tablespoons chopped fresh rosemary, leaves only
1 teaspoon rock salt or ¾ teaspoon kosher salt
¼ teaspoon freshly ground black pepper
8 cloves garlic, minced
½ cup olive oil
1 small ripe papaya

CABERNET SAUCE

1 large shallot, peeled and minced
1 cup Cabernet Sauvignon wine
¼ cup red wine vinegar
8 tablespoons (1 stick) unsalted butter,
  cold and cut into 6 pieces
¼ teaspoon kosher salt
¼ teaspoon freshly ground black pepper
1 tablespoon finely chopped fresh parsley leaves

PREPARE LAMB CHOPS

Rinse lamb chops in cold water, pat dry with paper towels and place in a large resealable plastic bag. Toast coriander seeds in a dry skillet over medium heat until just fragrant, watching carefully to prevent burning. When toasted seeds are cool, grind using a mortar and pestle or spice grinder, or crack by placing on a cutting board and crushing with a heavy cast iron skillet.

Place seeds in a small bowl. Add mustard, lemon juice, rosemary, salt, pepper, garlic and olive oil. Whisk to combine and pour marinade over bagged lamb chops. Seal the bag securely and massage the chops to coat with marinade. Marinate for 30 minutes at room temperature, or up to 4 hours in the refrigerator. While meat is marinating, prepare papaya.

PREPARE PAPAYA

Cut papaya in half lengthwise and scoop out seeds. Cut each half into ½-inch strips and peel skin from each strip. Chop each strip into ½-inch dice. Set aside; refrigerate if it will sit more than 1 hour.

PREPARE CABERNET SAUCE

Just before cooking lamb chops, prepare sauce. Place shallots, wine, and vinegar in a small saucepan. Mix well and reduce over medium-high heat to about 2 tablespoons of liquid. Reduce heat to medium-low. Slowly whisk in butter, one piece at a time. When all butter is added, cook for 30 seconds more. Remove from heat and add salt, pepper and parsley. Cover and keep warm over a very low flame or place in a 200-degree F oven.

COOK LAMB CHOPS

Heat a large cast iron or stainless steel skillet over high heat for 2 to 3 minutes. While the pan is heating, remove chops from marinade and drain by tapping lightly. Place chops in the skillet, head to tail, so each has plenty of room. Cook for about 3 minutes, turn and cook 3 minutes more for rare. Turn once or twice and cook up to 3 minutes more for medium.

ASSEMBLE

Arrange chops on a serving platter. Garnish with papaya and spoon sauce over all.

Kahua Ranch Lamb Curry

We created this dish when we started buying whole fresh lambs from Kahua Ranch. When that fragrant mix of island spices hits the pan, they give off a wonderful aroma, and the slow oven cooking tenderizes the meat. This is a stew that practically melts in your mouth. Without the optional cherry tomatoes, the curry is golden (as shown); with the tomatoes it turns to a beautiful red-orange. We serve it over basmati rice and top it with generous amounts of cilantro. For those who don't like cilantro, I suggest a simple pineapple-mint garnish (instructions at the end of the recipe). I also provide sambal oelek on the side for those who like to spice things up. Pair this curry with a fruity California Cabernet Sauvignon.

SERVES 6

LAMB

2½ pounds boneless lamb shoulder,
    cut into 1-inch cubes
1 tablespoon kosher salt
1 teaspoon cracked black pepper
2 teaspoons vegetable oil, divided

CURRY

1 teaspoon vegetable oil
2 teaspoons ground cumin
2 teaspoons ground cinnamon
2 teaspoons ground coriander
1 (2-inch) piece fresh ginger root,
    peeled and minced (about 2 tablespoons)
1 (2-3-inch) piece fresh turmeric,
    peeled and finely chopped (about 2 tablespoons)
    or 1 tablespoon dried ground turmeric
4 cloves garlic, minced
2 onions, quartered and sliced
1¼ cups water
1 (14.5-ounce) can coconut milk
½ fresh habanero pepper, seeded and finely
    chopped, or 2 teaspoons sambal oelek
2 cups cherry tomatoes (optional)

FOR ASSEMBLY

½ cup fresh cilantro leaves (optional)
1½ cups chopped fresh pineapple (optional)
4 sprigs fresh mint, leaves only,
    sliced chiffonade (optional)

PREPARE LAMB

Preheat the oven to 350 degrees F.

Place lamb cubes in a large bowl and toss with salt and pepper. Heat a Dutch oven to high, add 1 teaspoon of the vegetable oil and swirl gently to coat the bottom. Add half the lamb cubes and sear on all sides. Remove seared lamb to a plate, and repeat browning with 1 more teaspoon of the oil and the remaining lamb cubes.

PREPARE CURRY

Reduce heat to medium-high and add oil. Add cumin, cinnamon and coriander and sauté 1 minute. Add ginger, turmeric, garlic and onions. Sauté until onions begin to wilt, about 3 minutes. Add water and loosen brown crust on the bottom of the Dutch oven to deglaze. Add seared lamb, coconut milk, and habanero pepper. Stir to combine and bring to a boil. Cover and place in the oven for 50 minutes. Check lamb for tenderness; a fork should penetrate easily. If needed, cook 10 minutes more. Add cherry tomatoes, if using. Stir well, cover and return to the oven for another 20 minutes.

ASSEMBLE

Serve lamb curry over basmati rice and garnish each serving with cilantro leaves, if using. For pineapple-mint option: Just after adding cherry tomatoes to the curry, mix the chopped pineapple and mint chiffonade. When ready to serve, drain, and serve over curry or pass at the table.

Note: Turmeric is a natural dye that will temporarily stain your fingers yellow. With normal washing, it will disappear in a day or two. However, turmeric can leave a permanent stain on fabrics and hard surfaces, especially plastic, so be careful when handling.

Chinese-Style Braised Beef Short Ribs

These beef ribs are browned first, then braised v-e-r-y slowly until they're incredibly tender. If you can't find Chinese black vinegar, you can use 1¾ cups apple cider vinegar or sherry vinegar with ¼ cup of molasses added. We serve these ribs with hot mustard, white rice and spicy Watercress Kimchi (page 224).

SERVES 4

SHORT RIBS

5 pounds meaty bone-in beef short ribs
    (about 2 inches thick is ideal)
1½ tablespoons kosher salt
2 teaspoons freshly ground black pepper
3 tablespoons vegetable oil, divided

SAUCE

2–3 stalks celery, diced (about 1 cup)
2 leeks, white parts only,
    halved and diced (about 1 cup)
1 onion, diced (about 1 cup)
3–4 carrots, peeled and diced (about 1 cup)
2 cups Chinese black vinegar
½ cup honey
1 (6-ounce) can tomato paste
2 large cloves garlic, minced
1 (2-inch) piece fresh ginger root,
    peeled and minced (about 2 tablespoons)
½ cup soy sauce
1 tablespoon ground coriander
1 tablespoon ground star anise
Juice and zest of 1 orange
Juice and zest of 1 lime

PREPARE SHORT RIBS

Trim as much fat as possible from short ribs and season with salt and pepper.

In a large Dutch oven, heat 1 tablespoon of the vegetable oil for 30 seconds on medium-high heat. Brown about a third of the ribs, being careful not to crowd them. Allow each rib to brown completely on one side before turning, at least 2 minutes; they should lift easily off the pan without tearing. When ribs are browned on all sides, transfer to a plate. Repeat with remaining oil and ribs.

PREPARE SAUCE

Reduce heat to medium and add celery, leeks, onion and carrot to the remaining oil in the pot. Sauté vegetables, stirring often, until translucent, about 8 minutes. Add vinegar, honey, tomato paste, garlic, ginger, soy sauce, coriander, star anise, and citrus juices and zest to the pan. Stir to combine.

FINISH RIBS

Return ribs to the Dutch oven, submerging them in the liquid, adding water, if necessary, to just cover.

Turn heat to low and simmer, partially covered, for 2 to 3 hours until fork-tender and the liquid has reduced by 20 to 25 percent.

Transfer ribs to a clean plate. Refrigerate sauce for at least 2 hours. The recipe can be prepared to this point a day ahead, with the sauce and ribs refrigerated separately.

ASSEMBLE

Skim hardened fat from the sauce. Return ribs to the sauce and reheat over medium-low heat until just simmering.

Serve short ribs with just enough sauce to glaze the meat. Place extra sauce in a pitcher for passing at the table.

Option: To thicken the sauce before adding back the ribs, dissolve 3 tablespoons cornstarch in 2 tablespoons cold water. Bring sauce to a boil and stir in dissolved cornstarch. Return ribs to the sauce until warm.

Lamb Loin with Pineapple-Mint Chutney and Rosemary-Roasted Carrots

Rack of lamb is a restaurant menu staple, so it's familiar to most diners. Our tender, pan-roasted lamb loin has become a Merriman's Waimea favorite with regular customers. We developed this dish, which features spicy, oven-roasted carrots and cooling pineapple chutney with a hint of mint.

SERVES 4

ROASTED CARROTS

4–5 large carrots,
    peeled and cut into 2 x ¼-inch sticks
3 tablespoons chopped fresh rosemary,
    leaves only
⅜ teaspoon red pepper flakes
4 cloves garlic, thinly sliced
4 tablespoons canola oil
½ teaspoon kosher salt
¼ teaspoon freshly ground black pepper

PREPARE VEGETABLES

Preheat the oven to 425 degrees F. Use the roast or convection bake setting.

Place carrots, rosemary, pepper flakes, and garlic in a bowl and toss gently. Add canola oil, salt and pepper, and toss to coat vegetables with oil. Spread mixture onto a cookie sheet. Roast for 6 minutes, stir, and roast for 6 to 8 minutes more, until garlic is browned and carrots are lightly caramelized. Transfer cooked vegetables to a ceramic bowl and set aside. Reduce oven temperature to 350 degrees F.

LAMB

2-3 boneless lamb loins (about 2 pounds)
2 teaspoons table salt
½ teaspoon freshly ground black pepper
1½ tablespoons clarified butter (page 116)
1½ tablespoons unsalted butter
Pineapple-Mint Chutney

PREPARE LAMB

Each lamb loin will likely be in two pieces. Lay the smaller piece over the larger piece and tie together at each end using cotton string. Sprinkle lamb with salt and pepper. Heat a large, ovenproof skillet over medium-high heat for 2 minutes. Add clarified butter, swirling to coat, and add lamb. Brown for 2 minutes, roll meat a quarter turn and brown for 2 minutes more. Repeat 2 times more until all sides are well browned. Add unsalted butter to the skillet and, as it browns, baste meat with browning butter for about 1 minute. Place the skillet with lamb into the 350-degree F oven and roast for 10 to 15 minutes. Using an instant-read thermometer, check internal temperature: Cook to 145 degrees F for medium-rare, 160 degrees F for medium, and 170 degrees F for well-done. Remove the pan from the oven, transfer lamb to a cutting board and let rest for 4 minutes.

While lamb is resting, warm carrots in the oven or microwave. Remove string and slice each lamb loin into 6 pieces.

ASSEMBLE

Spread carrots onto a serving platter, placing lamb slices on top. Garnish with pineapple chutney and pass additional chutney at the table.

Pineapple-Mint Chutney

I'm not sure what the official difference is between chutney, relish and salsa, but chutneys are usually cooked and can be stored for a long time. This one is a fresh, barely cooked version. The sweet pineapple is perfect for cooling off the heat of the pepper flakes in the carrots. In addition to lamb, I also serve this chutney with grilled fish or shrimp.

MAKES ABOUT 2 CUPS

INGREDIENTS

½ *fresh pineapple, peeled, cored*
    and cut into ¼*-inch dice*
¼ *sweet onion, cut into* ¼*-inch dice (about* ¼ *cup)*
1 (1-inch) piece fresh ginger root,
    peeled and minced
½ *cup rice wine vinegar*
⅜ *cup light brown sugar*
¼ *teaspoon nam pla*
1 tablespoon chopped fresh mint
½ *tablespoon orange zest*

PREPARATION

Place pineapple, onion and ginger into a stainless steel or ceramic bowl and stir gently to combine. Measure vinegar and brown sugar into a small saucepan, stir, and bring to a boil over medium-high heat. Remove the pan from the heat and stir in nam pla. While liquid is still very hot, pour it over pineapple mixture and stir to coat fruit. Cover and chill 3 to 24 hours. Twenty minutes prior to serving, remove chutney from the refrigerator, and stir in mint and orange zest. Just before serving, drain liquid from chutney using a strainer.

Rules for Cooking Steak (and other red meats)

Rule #1: Liberally season meat on both sides.

I often use dry rubs, but you cannot go wrong with a simple mix of large grain salt and freshly ground black pepper in a 8:1 ratio.

Rule #2: Whether you are grilling or pan-frying, preheat the metal cooking surface over high heat.

You want the meat to sear quickly and form a dark, crusty exterior. The darkening color means the protein in the meat is caramelizing. This helps to prevent the meat from sticking to the grill or pan, makes it look more appetizing and develops the rich flavor.

If you are using a charcoal grill, don't skimp on the charcoal. Wait until the coals are white hot, then heat the grilling surface, with the grill cover on, for at least 5 minutes. For a gas grill, heat on high with the top down for at least 15 minutes. For pan-frying, use a heavy skillet and heat on high for at least 3 minutes before adding the meat.

Rule #3: There are no actual rules about how long to cook the meat because the timing is dependent upon 3 variables:

• How hot is your cooking surface?
• How thick is the meat?
• How well do you want the meat cooked?

We use resistance to determine doneness.

DONENESS	RESISTANCE	FEELS LIKE
Rare	Soft	Touching your cheek
Medium	Moderate resistance	Touching the end of your nose
Well-done	Lots of resistance	Pressing on your chin bone

I aim for 3 to 4 minutes on each side with 1-inch-thick steaks for rare, 5 to 6 minutes for medium-rare, and longer for thicker steaks.

Pipikaula (Beef Smoke Meat)

Smoke meat is everywhere in Hawai'i. Most of it is smoked at very low temperatures (low and slow) and the vast majority of smoke meat on the islands uses wild pig. The result is similar to what many folks consider jerky. When made with beef, smoke meat is called pipikaula (pipi means cow; kaula means rope), and it is typically served as an appetizer (pupu). We slice our pipikaula into bite-size pieces, heat it up in a frying pan, and serve it alongside some cold green bottles. *Note:* This recipe requires overnight refrigeration to marinate before cooking.

SERVES 8 TO 10 AS AN APPETIZER

INGREDIENTS
1 teaspoon liquid smoke
½ cup dark brown sugar
½ cup soy sauce
2 pounds flank steak
1 tablespoon freshly grated ginger root
2 large cloves garlic, minced
*   (about 1 tablespoon)*
1½ teaspoons sea salt or kosher salt
½ teaspoon coarsely ground black pepper

PREPARE AND MARINATE BEEF
Combine liquid smoke, brown sugar and soy sauce in a bowl and stir until sugar is dissolved. Cut flank steak lengthwise, with the grain, into 1-inch-wide strips. Place in a shallow plastic container or glass dish and pour liquid over the meat. Cover with a lid or plastic wrap and refrigerate overnight.

COOK PIPIKAULA
Preheat the oven to 200 degrees F.

Remove beef from marinade and place on an oiled rack in a sheet pan (lined with foil for easier cleanup). Discard marinade. Mix ginger, garlic, salt and pepper in a small bowl. Sprinkle half of the mixture evenly over beef. Turn beef and sprinkle with the remaining seasoning mixture. Place beef in the oven and bake for 3 hours, turning once after 1 hour and 30 minutes. The beef should be dry but still flexible. Remove from the oven and let cool on the rack. Store in refrigerator in a tightly closed plastic bag or container for up to 1 month.

ASSEMBLE
To serve, cut into bite-size pieces, and heat gently in a frying pan.

Range-Fed Beef and Wine Stew

In its first incarnation, Merriman's Waimea was a casual bistro and this version of beef bourguignon, showcasing home-grown range-fed beef, was a menu star. My friend Pono Von Holt, a local rancher, taught me that cattle ranching is mostly about grass farming. The trick to raising cattle is growing the right grass to feed them and then moving them around the pasture to manage the grass supply. As Merriman's focus shifted to more of a fine-dining restaurant, we kept serving that great grass-fed beef, but the stew eventually came off the menu. Still, it remains one of my favorite dishes. *Note:* This recipe requires overnight dry marinating prior to cooking.

SERVES 6 TO 8

BEEF

2½ pounds grass-fed chuck roast,
cut into 1-inch cubes

1½ tablespoons kosher salt

1 teaspoon freshly ground black pepper

4 sprigs fresh rosemary

4 sprigs fresh thyme

2 tablespoons coarsely chopped fresh thyme

4 sprigs fresh flat-leaf parsley

1 large white onion, chopped into ½-inch squares

STEW

4 ounces salt pork, rind removed,
cut into ½-inch cubes

3 cloves garlic, thinly sliced

¼ cup all-purpose flour

2 cups inexpensive red wine
(Shiraz or Pinot Noir work well)

3 carrots, peeled and cut into ½-inch pieces

3 stalks celery, cut into ¼-inch pieces

8 ounces fresh button or cremini mushrooms,
stemmed and quartered

2 tablespoons butter

½ pound fresh green beans,
trimmed and cut into 1-inch lengths

DRY MARINATE BEEF

Place beef in a large bowl or plastic container, toss with salt, pepper, rosemary, thyme (both), parsley and onion. Cover and refrigerate at least overnight and up to 24 hours.

PREPARE STEW

Preheat the oven to 325 degrees F.

Transfer beef cubes to a bowl, shaking off most of the herbs and discarding parsley. Transfer onion to a separate bowl. Reserve remaining herbs.

Place pork in a Dutch oven over medium-high heat. As the fat renders, add half the beef cubes (or as many as will fit without crowding) and sear until dark brown. Remove to a plate and continue browning process with remaining beef.

Place onions in the Dutch oven, reduce heat to medium and cook until translucent, about 3 minutes. Return beef to the Dutch oven. Add garlic and reserved herbs. Add flour and stir for 2 to 3 minutes until completely absorbed (no flour should be visible). Add red wine and stir well, loosening browned bits on the bottom to deglaze the pan. Bring mixture to a boil, cover and place in the oven. Cook for 1½ hours. Add carrots and celery, stir and cook 30 minutes more. Meat should be fork-tender. If needed, cook an additional 15 minutes to desired degree of doneness. Stew can be cooked to this point up to 48 hours prior to serving and refrigerated.

ASSEMBLE

In a skillet, sauté mushrooms in butter over medium-high heat until just beginning to brown. Stir cooked mushrooms and uncooked green beans into the stew and cook in the oven for 15 minutes more. If finishing after refrigeration, add cooked mushrooms and uncooked green beans to the stew, stirring well, and place in a 350-degree F oven for 30 to 40 minutes. Stir every 10 minutes until stew is heated through.

Serve stew over egg noodles or with crusty bread—or both.

Citrus Pepper Steak

I love grass-fed beef. There is no grain. Virtually all Hawai'i beef is pasture finished. For this dish, it's well worth buying grass-fed steaks, if you have a good supplier. My favorite cut for this dish is a ribeye. We developed this recipe using several different kinds of pepper—cayenne, red pepper flakes and black pepper—and the fat in the butter helps blend them. (Use grass-fed butter, too, if you can.) The big surprise is the citrus.

SERVES 4

CITRUS BUTTER
8 tablespoons (1 stick) unsalted butter, softened
¼ teaspoon cayenne pepper
Zest of ½ lemon
Zest of ⅓ orange
2 tablespoons soy sauce

1 (8-inch-wide) sheet wax paper or plastic wrap

STEAK
1 tablespoon kosher salt
2 teaspoons red pepper flakes
1 tablespoon coriander seeds
2 teaspoons coarsely ground black pepper
4 steaks, any cut

PREPARE CITRUS BUTTER
Using an electric mixer, beat softened butter and add cayenne pepper and lemon and orange zests. Add soy sauce, 1 tablespoon at a time, mixing well after each addition. Scoop butter onto wax paper or plastic wrap and shape into a log about 4 inches long. Roll wrapping around the seasoned butter. Refrigerate 2 hours or up to 2 weeks. Remove from the refrigerator 30 minutes prior to serving.

PREPARE GRILL
If using a gas grill, preheat on high with the lid down for 20 minutes. If using charcoal, light the grill 30 to 45 minutes before cooking; once the flames are gone, test it periodically. It's ready when you can't hold the back of your hand over the heat for 5 seconds.

COOK STEAK
In a small bowl, mix kosher salt, red pepper flakes, coriander seed and black pepper. When the grill is ready, rub spice mix onto both sides of each steak. Grill steaks to desired degree of doneness. (See Rules for Cooking Steak, page 144.)

ASSEMBLE
Distribute steaks among 4 plates. Cut citrus butter into 8 equal portions, and overlap 2 pieces per steak.

The Schwenker Grill

SIT ON THE BENCH outside Merriman's Waimea and you'll see the arriving customers stop as they get out of their cars and look around for the source of the aromas of smoke and roasting meat. It only takes a few seconds to spot the schwenker. We heard a story about schwenkers on NPR and decided to get one. These swinging grills, which originated in the Mosel Valley of Germany, are pushed back and forth over the coals while cooks and guests enjoy beer and conversation. The larger the chunks of meat, the longer the cooking time—and the more beer gets consumed. Neil Murphy said Waimea reminded him of the German countryside—brooding mountains, green hills, wind, blue sky, and sheep. I liked the idea of a grill in the courtyard, so we went to see Ethan Froney who works as a blacksmith at Anna's Ranch in Waimea. He was intrigued and agreed to forge the first and only schwenker in Hawai'i. We use kiawe wood in the fire bowl and the foods develop smoky, fire-roasted flavors that are unmatched. Merriman's Chef Neil Murphy developed some fabulous recipes using hog, lamb, goat, beef, whole fish, and all kinds of vegetables. So grab a beer, come sit in the courtyard and enjoy the magic of the schwenker.

Steak with Shoyu-Roasted Mushrooms

The mushrooms are the real stars of this dish. Any kind will work, but we like to use a mix of different varieties. As they roast, the salty shoyu (soy sauce) brings out their natural earthiness and they take on a soft chewy texture, with just a little kick from the red pepper flakes. I love them with hanger steak, which is also known as skirt steak. Perhaps the most flavorful and tender of all steaks, it used to be called butcher's steak because the butcher often kept it aside for himself.

SERVES 4

MUSHROOMS

¼ cup soy sauce

½ cup olive oil

3 cloves garlic, sliced

1 teaspoon red pepper flakes

3 cups sliced mushrooms

STEAK

1½ –2 pounds hanger steak, cut into 4 pieces

1 teaspoon table salt

½ teaspoon freshly ground black pepper

1 avocado,

* peeled and sliced lengthwise into 8 pieces*

1 lime, quartered

PREPARE MUSHROOMS

Preheat the oven to 450 degrees F.

Combine soy sauce, olive oil, garlic and red pepper flakes in a bowl. Add mushrooms, mix thoroughly, and let sit for 5 minutes to absorb some of the marinade. Using a slotted spoon, remove mushrooms and spread evenly in a roasting pan. Reserve the marinade. Roast mushrooms for 5 to 6 minutes, until cooked and just barely browned.

COOK STEAK

Heat a cast iron skillet over high heat for at least 3 minutes. Season steaks with salt and pepper. Cook to desired degree of donenesss, about 4 minutes each side. (See Rules for Cooking Steak, page 144.) Transfer to a serving platter.

ASSEMBLE

Return the skillet to the stovetop; over medium heat add mushroom marinade. Add mushrooms and stir, heating for just 1 to 2 minutes. Spoon warm mushrooms over steaks, top each steak with 2 slices avocado, and squeeze lime over avocado.

Ulapalakua Beef and Shrimp Kabobs

This recipe was named for the Ulapalakua Ranch, one of the largest on Maui. These are simple kabobs made special by the inclusion of pineapple and a killer sauce. We put the shrimp versus the beef on separate skewers because they require different cooking times. Make smaller kabobs, serve with a separate dipping sauce, and you have a quick-to-prepare appetizer. Or make larger kabobs, serve them with some rice and pour on the sauce for a main course that easily expands with your guest list. Make the dipping sauce first so it's ready when the kabobs are hot.

MAKES 12 KABOBS, 6 SHRIMP AND 6 BEEF

DIPPING SAUCE
2 tablespoons freshly grated ginger root
½ cup brown sugar
½ cup soy sauce
¼ cup rice wine vinegar
2 tablespoons toasted sesame oil
2 tablespoons scallions,
    green parts only, thinly sliced

SHRIMP AND BEEF KABOBS
(U-16/20 count), peeled and deveined
1½ pounds boneless New York strip steak,
    cut into 1-inch cubes
¼ cup brown sugar
1 tablespoon coarsely ground black pepper
1 tablespoon kosher salt
½ fresh pineapple, peeled,
    cored and cut into ½-inch cubes
1 sweet onion, cut into 1-inch squares
1–2 red bell peppers, cut into 1-inch squares
Vegetable oil

18 bamboo skewers, presoaked in water

PREPARE SAUCE
Mix all ingredients in a bowl and set aside.

PREPARE BEEF AND SHRIMP
Place shrimp and cubed beef into separate shallow bowls or pie plates. In a small bowl, combine brown sugar, black pepper and kosher salt. Sprinkle half the seasoning over shrimp and toss to coat; sprinkle remaining half over beef and toss to coat.

ASSEMBLE KABOBS
Assemble the kabobs by alternating pineapple, onion and peppers with either shrimp or beef. When threading shrimp, push the skewer point through the back and then through the tail so each shrimp lies flat and cooks more evenly.

COOK KABOBS
Heat the grill, then oil it or coat with cooking spray. Grill kabobs for 3 to 7 minutes per side (you want nice grill marks without overcooking). Shrimp are done when they turn pink. Beef can be cooked to desired degree of doneness.

  Note: To oil your grill, place a few tablespoons vegetable oil in a bowl. Crumple a paper towel, pick up with tongs, dip in the oil and wipe the grill.

Kona Coffee-Rubbed Lamb Loin with Spicy Mint Dipping Sauce

This coffee rub works well on beef or lamb. If lamb loins are hard to find, you can use other cuts of lamb. The trick is to start with the best-quality lamb you can find, and then don't overcook the meat. For side dishes, I like roasted carrots and Swiss chard or whatever vegetables are in season, and we often garnish with pineapple chunks. This lamb also inspired the creation of an unusual, spicy mint dipping sauce.

SERVES 4

LAMB

4 (6-ounce) pieces boneless lamb loin

2 tablespoons kosher salt

1 tablespoon finely ground dark roast Kona coffee

1 teaspoon ground cinnamon

2 teaspoons fresh thyme leaves

1 teaspoon freshly ground black pepper

2 tablespoons vegetable oil

PREPARE LAMB

Tie up lamb loins into neat logs using kitchen string. Combine salt, coffee, cinnamon, thyme and pepper in a small bowl. Coat lamb with coffee rub. Heat a cast iron skillet or heavy-bottomed pan on high heat for 1 to 2 minutes. Add oil, gently swirling to coat the pan. Cook lamb for 3 minutes per side, 12 minutes total. Remove lamb to a cutting board, cut string and let rest about 5 minutes before slicing. Serve with individual bowls of mint dipping sauce on the side.

SPICY MINT DIPPING SAUCE

3 cloves garlic, roughly chopped

3/8 cup granulated sugar

1/2 habanero pepper, seeded and minced, or 1 tablespoon sambal oelek

1/2 cup rice wine vinegar

1/2 cup fresh mint leaves

1/4 cup fresh flat-leaf parsley leaves

1/2 teaspoon salt

1/2 cup olive oil

PREPARE DIPPING SAUCE

In a blender or food processor, grind sugar, garlic and habanero. Add vinegar and process until the sugar dissolves. Add mint, parsley and salt and process with 5 (3-second) pulses. With the motor running, drizzle in oil and blend for 5 seconds after all oil is added.

CHAPTER 5

Pig Is King

Dave Fitch—
Malama Farm

DAVE FITCH HAS A MESSAGE for anyone interested in raising pigs using a small scale, humane, rotational pasture model—it works! At the end of the day, Dave and his wife, Lehua, sometimes can't believe what they did that morning, like helping hogs mate, or castrating some of the males. "We're basically city folk, but our lives definitely have a bit of a *Green Acres* quality," Dave says.

Dave and Lehua moved from San Francisco to Maui in 2009 to raise heritage Berkshire hogs (also known as Kurobuta pork). They had never been farmers but wanted their children to grow up in a more rural setting. Why pigs? "We developed a fondness for them while traveling in New Zealand," Dave told me. "They're really hilarious—kolohe (rascals). If you're fixing some machinery and a pig is nearby, don't be surprised if your wrench disappears!"

Malama Farm's hogs live pampered lives. Their pastures are constantly renewed by chickens following the hogs, feasting on the bugs living in the waste left behind, and in turn renewing the nitrogen in the soil with their own waste. It's a method designed to live up to the farm's name, Malama, which means to care for, nurture, preserve.

"We'd like to see Hawai'i continue to reduce its reliance on imported food, and we think this model for raising livestock on a small scale is one way to do that," Dave told me. I love that idea, and I'm really glad we can serve Malama Farm's pork in our restaurants.

Kalua Pork Imu-Style at Home

Some of the old ways of Hawai'i remain in the local culture. One of my favorites is barter. Most communities have *the guy* who is really good at making imus. Friends will call on him to help when making a luau. Rick Gordon made the imu for my kids' luau. In return, some smoked meat, fresh-caught fish or fruit from your yard is appreciated. Most important, you have to stay awake all night and make certain the imu doesn't burn. This requires a hose, a shovel, a lot of beer and a bit of bourbon.

Kalua refers to cooking in an earthen oven in the ground (imu). With this recipe, you get the same succulent pork without the pit. I still think it's a good idea to drink some beer while it roasts. Serve it with rice or in a sandwich. Either way, kalua pork goes well with Pineapple Cole Slaw (page 69) or Watercress Kimchi (page 224) and kalua pork tacos are killer good! *Note:* This recipe includes overnight dry marinating prior to cooking.

SERVES 6

PORK

1 (5–6 pound) pork shoulder
    (also known as Boston butt or pork butt)
2 tablespoons kosher salt
2 tablespoons brown sugar
3 teaspoons red pepper flakes
    or crushed red pepper, divided
3 large sweet onions
1½ tablespoons olive oil
¾ teaspoon liquid smoke

PREPARE PORK A DAY AHEAD

Separate pork butt into 4 to 5 large chunks, removing excess fat on the surface and between the muscles. In a small bowl, mix salt, sugar and 2 teaspoons of the pepper flakes. Rub mixture over the pork to coat. Place pork into a bowl or casserole dish, cover with plastic wrap or a tight lid and refrigerate overnight.

ROAST PORK

Preheat the oven to 250 degrees F. Use the roast setting, if available.

Cut onions in half lengthwise and slice into ¼-inch pieces. In a large skillet, heat olive oil over medium heat for 15 seconds. Add onions and remaining red pepper flakes. Cook slowly, at least 10 minutes, stirring often and lowering the heat if necessary, until onions are caramelized to a light tan color. Stir in liquid smoke.

In a heavy Dutch oven, place pork pieces and onion mixture in layers. Cover and roast for 4 to 5 hours, until meat is fork-tender. Remove from the oven and let sit, covered, in the pot to cool. When meat is cool enough to handle easily, transfer to a cutting board, leaving the cooking liquid in the pot. Slice pork with a knife, or shred it using your fingers.

Pour cooking liquid into a 1-quart measuring cup or bowl. Skim as much fat as possible, or chill liquid for 3 hours, then skim the hardened fat. If more than 1 cup of liquid remains, return to the pot and boil to reduce to 1 cup, and reserve. Use reserved liquid to moisten meat when serving kalua pork on its own or in sandwiches. Both meat and liquid can be stored in the refrigerator for 1 week or frozen for several months.

Pork Bulgogi Tacos by Monkeypod Kitchen by Merriman

Bulgogi is basically spicy, marinated grilled meat. Traditional Korean bulgogi is made with beef, and you can certainly substitute skirt steak for the pork in this recipe, but in Hawai'i we love pork. A key to this preparation is slicing the pork into very narrow strips because the meat must be thin to cook properly yet remain tender. At both Monkeypod Kitchen by Merriman and Moku, we serve our tacos with a refreshing Asian pear and some kimchi on the side.

PORK BULGOGI TACOS

½ cup brown sugar

1 tablespoon sambal oelek

1 tablespoon nam pla or nuoc mam

1 (1-inch) piece fresh ginger root, minced (about 1 tablespoon)

4 large cloves garlic, minced (about 2 tablespoons)

½ cup soy sauce

2 teaspoons toasted sesame oil

1 pound boneless pork loin, cut into ½-inch strips

1 tablespoon vegetable oil

½ onion, thinly sliced

4 sprigs fresh cilantro or more if you love it

12 corn or flour tortillas

OPTIONAL FIXINGS

1 Asian pear, peeled, diced or matchstick cut

Scallions, white and green parts, thinly sliced

Fresh jalapeño peppers, sliced into thin rounds

Watercress Kimchi (page 224)

Sour cream

PREPARE PORK BULGOGI

Mix sugar, sambal oelek, nam pla, ginger, garlic, soy sauce and sesame oil in a large bowl. Add meat and refrigerate for 1 to 4 hours. Remove meat from marinade and place in a colander to drain excess liquid. Reserve marinade.

Heat a sauté pan over high heat for 1 minute. Add vegetable oil, swirling pan to coat, and immediately add pork. Stir-fry for 1 to 2 minutes, add onions and stir-fry for 1 or 2 minutes more, until onions are well wilted.

PREPARE EXTRA SAUCE

Remove meat and onions from the pan, reduce heat to medium-high and add marinade. Bring to a boil, and reduce by about 25 percent to use as additional sauce, if desired.

ASSEMBLE

Warm tortillas in the oven or microwave, or toast in a nonstick skillet. Place a portion of the pork in the center of a warm tortilla and garnish with cilantro, plus any other fixings you like.

Goat Cheese–Crusted Pork Chops

Use the best quality pork chops you can find for this dish. We use Berkshire (Kurobuta) pork from Malama Farm on Maui's north shore. Berskshires are a breed of black pig originally from the county of Berkshire just west of London in England. Highly prized in Japan, they are raised in the Kagoshima prefecture under the trademarked named of Kagoshima Kurobuta pork. In this dish, the combination of creamy goat cheese and macadamia nuts with a deeply flavored wine sauce really highlights the pork, which is cooked in a high-temperature oven after a quick sear to keep it super moist.

SERVES 4

GOAT CHEESE CRUST

8 ounces fresh goat cheese (preferably chèvre)

*½ cup dry-roasted macadamia nuts,
    broken or chopped into large pieces*

1 clove garlic, minced

1 tablespoon chopped fresh dill

2 teaspoons chopped fresh rosemary

PORK CHOPS

*4 (5–6-ounce) pork loin chops,
    about ¾-inch thick*

1 teaspoon salt

½ teaspoon freshly ground black pepper

1 tablespoon vegetable oil

SAUCE

1 tablespoon olive oil

½ cup shallots, sliced

8 ounces button mushrooms, quartered

1½ cups red wine

½ cup tomato, chopped

3 tablespoons butter, cold and cut into 3 pieces

*½ cup fresh flat-leaf parsley, roughly chopped,
    for garnish*

PREPARE CRUSTED CHOPS

Preheat the oven to 475 degrees F.

Using a fork, mash together goat cheese, nuts, garlic, dill and rosemary in a bowl, and set aside.

Heat a heavy skillet over high heat for at least 1 minute. Season chops with salt and pepper. Add vegetable oil to the skillet and sear chops on each side, about 1 minute per side. Remove chops to a baking pan, but reserve the skillet and pan drippings for the sauce. Spread one quarter of the goat cheese mixture evenly over each chop. Place chops in the oven for 12 minutes.

PREPARE SAUCE

While chops are roasting, prepare the sauce. Add olive oil, shallots and mushrooms into the hot skillet with pan drippings. Sauté over medium-high heat until mushrooms start to soften, about 2 minutes. Add wine, increase heat to high, and reduce sauce by one-third. Add tomatoes, and cook 1 minute. Gently stir in butter, 1 piece at a time. Remove the skillet from the heat and cover until ready to serve.

ASSEMBLE

Divide sauce into equal portions among 4 plates, place chops on top of sauce and sprinkle with parsley.

JK's Smokehouse

JK SPIELMAN AND I HAVE BEEN FRIENDS since we worked at the Mauna Lani Resort and paddled at Kawaihae Canoe Club. JK grew up on Oʻahu, but his family spent summers at their cottage on Paniau Beach on the Big Island.

Lucky for his family and friends, JK smokes meat in the immaculate private smokehouse he built with his brother in Waimea. He only uses dried kiawe wood, and starts with locally raised, hormone-free meat. His secret is a hot, quick smoke—just two hours or so—rather than a longer, lower temperature smoke. "It helps retain the inherent flavor of the meat, keeps it moist, and assures it's not overly smoky," he told me.

JK likes to place a pork belly on a flat rack over the hanging meat, so the fat drips down for more flavor. He vacuum seals and freezes the result, then gifts it to a lucky few.

Want to serve smoked meat JK-style? Fry it in a skillet with a splash of soy sauce and a touch of homemade poha jam. So ono. Folks who like to smoke meat are generally known for the quality of their product. You'll hear Waimea folks say, "JK makes the best smoked meat!"

Pork Adobo

I first tasted pork adobo at a potluck after a canoe regatta. I knew if I ever had my own restaurant, I wanted to serve flavors like this—bold, complex and yet so well blended they seemed comforting and familiar. We don't actually serve pork adobo in the restaurant, but I make it often for family and friends and use the flavor profile in any number of other restaurant dishes. Here we put the pork on a bed of fresh spinach for a bit of color, but in Hawai'i you will only see pork adobo served with short-grain white rice, also called sticky rice. I love a cool, crunchy side dish, like kimchi or Pineapple Cole Slaw (page 69).

SERVES 4

PORK AND SAUCE

1 ½ pounds pork shoulder
   (also known as Boston butt or pork butt)
¼ cup soy sauce
1 cup water
½ cup cider vinegar
2 bay leaves
1 tablespoon coriander seeds, crushed
½ teaspoon ground cumin
1 teaspoon paprika
1 tablespoon whole black peppercorns
2 teaspoons table salt
½ teaspoon freshly ground black pepper
2 tablespoons vegetable or canola oil, divided
5–6 large cloves garlic, minced
   (about 3 tablespoons)
½ cup onions, chopped

FOR ASSEMBLY

Juice of ½ lemon
1 cup fresh cilantro leaves, roughly chopped

MARINATE PORK

Remove and discard large pieces of fat from pork. Cut pork into 1-inch cubes. Place pork cubes into a resealable plastic bag and place bag into a bowl. In a separate bowl, mix soy sauce, water and vinegar. Divide the liquid into 2 equal portions. Set 1 portion aside. Add the other portion to the pork, close and seal the bag, and knead gently to ensure pork is thoroughly drenched with marinade. Marinate in the refrigerator for 4 to 8 hours. Marinating longer will mean more flavor in the final dish.

COOK PORK

Add bay leaves, coriander seeds, cumin, paprika, and peppercorns to reserved soy sauce-vinegar mixture, and set aside.

Remove pork from marinating liquid, drain, and dry cubes on paper towels. Discard marinade. Heat a heavy skillet with a tight-fitting lid on high heat for 1 to 2 minutes. Season drained pork with salt and pepper. Add 1 tablespoon of the oil to the skillet, and brown about half

Recipe continued on page 174

Recipe continued from page 172
of the pork. Don't crowd the pan. Turn pork cubes individually so each piece is nicely browned on all sides. (See note below.) Remove browned pork to a plate, and repeat the browning process using remaining oil, until all pork is browned. (You may need to reduce the heat to medium-high to avoid burning.) Return all pork to the skillet. Add garlic and cook on high heat until garlic is golden brown. Lower heat to medium, add onions and cook for 1 minute. Add reserved spicy soy sauce-vinegar liquid, cover and bring to a boil. Reduce heat and simmer for 20 minutes. Stir and if pork is getting dry, add ½ cup water. Continue to simmer, covered, until pork is fork-tender, about 20 minutes more.

ASSEMBLE

Remove the pan from the heat, add lemon juice and stir to combine. Place in a large bowl to serve family style and sprinkle with cilantro.

Note: Browning the pork is a critical step. The pan must be hot, and heavy enough that it won't lose too much heat when the meat is added. Using tongs, place pork cubes one at a time, leaving space between and turning each piece individually. Wait for each side to brown before turning so that all sides are evenly browned. Yes, this takes longer than stirring, but that's cooking with aloha.

Monkeypod Kitchen by Merriman, Wailea, Maui

The Infamous Cheese Raid

IN THE FIRST YEAR after Merriman's Waimea opened, I worked some very long hours. One Saturday, I was standing at the sink peeling and deveining endless pounds of shrimp when a couple of hippies pushed open the kitchen door. Steve Sayre, lean and tall with shoulder-length brown hair, and his wife, Karin, in a colorful skirt and peasant blouse, her long hair tied back with a piece of leather, waited politely. While I washed my hands, they explained they were goat farmers from Puna, a backcountry town in the southeast corner of the Big Island, about halfway between Hilo and Kilauea, and they wanted to sell me some cheese. It only took a few min-

utes of conversation to see that these very nice people were also smart, knowledgeable and passionate about making high-quality handcrafted goat cheese.

I dried my hands and took the sample they offered. I'll never forget the lightly pungent tang combined with the smoothest texture I'd ever tasted. I placed an order for several pounds, or as much as they could produce. Then they told me it was their very first order. I asked where else they had stopped on the hour-and-a-half drive from Puna. "We didn't stop anywhere," Steve replied. "We are proud of our cheese, and we want it served in the best restaurant." Of course, I was flattered.

As soon as the first order arrived, it was an instant hit. Our head-waiter, Guy Suzuki, proudly announced to customers that Merriman's was the only place serving Hawai'i-made goat cheese in the world.

A short time later, after stories about locally produced goat cheese began to appear in the newspapers and tourist magazines, we were raided. Someone from the Hawai'i Department of Health read the stories and realized that no permits had been issued to any cheese makers in Puna.

As the health department enforcers came through Merriman's front door, Chef Sandy Barr stuffed as much of the Sayre's goat cheese as she could into a can of olive oil back in the kitchen. (Little did she know that the lightly marinated cheese would turn out to be a wonderful gastronomic technique!)

In the months that followed, and with encouragement from me and a number of Merriman's regulars, the Department of Health showed that they could be visionary—in fact, they went from enforcing to supporting—working closely with Steve and Karin, and issuing the first-ever health permit for cheese made with water from a catchment system. And it didn't stop there. The Health Department teamed up with the Department of Agriculture to help the Sayres get a State of Hawai'i loan so they could increase their herd and begin supplying other restaurants in the state featuring Hawai'i Regional Cuisine. Now that's aloha spirit!

I never thought a raid could have such a happy ending.

Pickled Pineapple Roast Pork

We had to take this off the menu in Waimea because I gained 15 pounds. This is one of my favorite ways to cook and eat pork shoulder. It is slightly sweet, slightly sour, with just a hint of spicy heat. In addition to white or brown rice, I suggest serving it with some sautéed mustard greens, or Swiss chard. It also goes well with Monkeypod Kitchen Kale Salad (page 82).

SERVES 6

PORK ROAST
1 (3-pound) boneless pork shoulder roast, trimmed of excess fat and tied or netted
1 tablespoon red pepper flakes
1 tablespoon coarsely chopped fresh rosemary
1 tablespoon kosher salt
2 cloves garlic, minced

PICKLED PINEAPPLE
1 fresh pineapple, peeled and cored
½ cup rice wine vinegar
½ cup dark brown sugar
8 whole cloves
1 large shallot, chopped
1 tablespoon flour
2 cups chicken stock
¼ cup dark rum (optional)

PREPARE PORK
Preheat the oven to 325 degrees F. Use the roast setting, if available

Using a paper towel, pat roast dry. Mix red pepper flakes, rosemary, salt and garlic in a small bowl. Rub mixture over pork to coat, not missing any nooks and crannies in the meat. Place seasoned pork in a large roasting pan and roast for approximately 1½ hours.

PREPARE PINEAPPLE
While pork is roasting, cut pineapple in half lengthwise, then slice each half lengthwise into 3 wedges. Place pineapple wedges in a shallow glass baking dish. Mix vinegar, brown sugar and cloves in a small bowl and pour over pineapple. Using tongs, turn pineapple until well coated with seasonings. Microwave on high for 2 minutes.

FINISH PORK
Check pork with an instant-read thermometer after 1 hour; continue roasting, as needed, until center temperature reaches 160 degrees F. Transfer roast to a plate or cutting board, cover with foil and let rest, still tied (it will be easier to slice when cool). Increase oven temperature to 475 degrees F.

FINISH PINEAPPLE
Remove pineapple wedges from vinegar mixture and set aside. Strain vinegar mixture to remove cloves and reserve the liquid. Lay pineapple flat on the bottom of the roasting pan and roast in the oven for 6 to 7 minutes, until nicely browned. Transfer to the plate with the pork. Slice pineapple into smaller pieces or keep them whole, as you wish.

Place the roasting pan on the stovetop over medium-high heat. Stir in shallots and flour, whisking continuously, until flour is fully absorbed into the fat and brown in color, about 4 minutes.

Add ¼ cup of the reserved vinegar mixture and bring to a boil, scraping the bottom of the pan to deglaze. Add chicken stock, bring back to a boil and cook until the sauce thickens. Turn off heat and stir in rum, if using.

ASSEMBLE
Cut away string, slice pork, and serve with pineapple. Drizzle sauce over all. Pass extra sauce at the table.

First-Birthday Luau

ONE OF MY FAVORITE Hawaiian traditions is the first-birthday luau. This special feast celebrates the survival of a child's perilous first year of life and, in older times, included his or her official naming ritual.

Vicki and I had first-birthday luaus for each of our three children (now twenty-six, twenty-three and twenty years old). Cody is our first-born and his luau took place in the backyard of our tiny house in Puako. Merriman's

Waimea had been open barely a year and the staff were stretched thin, so I did all the cooking myself. I stayed up all night to roast the pig and make shoyu chicken, lomi lomi salmon, lau lau, baked sweet potatoes, and fruit salad—just me and a few beers. I think our 'ohana enjoyed the party, but I pretty much sleep-walked through it.

Three years later, we were planning the luau for our daughter Ivy. We had a little more money by this time, so we rented the Spencer Pavilion in Kawaihae (and Rick Gordon made the imu). It's right next to the cooks' quarters where I lived when I first came to Hawai'i and down the road from the canoe club. I started on the Shrimp Luau

(recipe on page 48). Nowadays even native Hawaiians would probably use canned coconut milk for this soup, but I wanted everything to be as authentic as possible, so I grabbed a huge knife to clean some fresh coconuts. Just minutes later, I put the knife right through my hand. I just wrapped it up and kept cooking. (Every time I tell this story, I can feel a tingling where I probably severed a nerve or two.)

Three more years and it was time for a third luau for our daughter Jessie. We were finally gaining some financial stability—the Waimea restaurant was doing well, and we had moved to Maui so I could open Hula Grill Maui. Jessie's luau was held at the clubhouse at Puamana,

right on the ocean. We hired a couple of cooks and some waitstaff. What a difference! I enjoyed the party well-rested, unbandaged and in a great mood. Vicki and I stood at the edge of the crowd, sharing a beer. I told her we had finally nailed the first-birthday luau, so I was ready for more kids. I'm not sure what she was thinking, but she just smiled her beautiful smile, quietly said "I don't think so," and walked away carrying Jessie on her hip.

Kalua Pork and Maui Onion Quesadillas with Mango-Chili Dipping Sauce

These are a huge favorite at all the restaurants. Maybe it's because they are easy to share as an appetizer, or because the sweet-hot dipping sauce is tasty enough to eat by itself with a spoon, or because quesadillas are a basic comfort food for kids, grownups and everyone in between. I like to think it is because they are just sooo good!

MAKES 4 QUESADILLAS

INGREDIENTS
8 (8-inch) flour tortillas
4 tablespoons fresh goat cheese
1½ cups Kalua Pork, including onions (page 164)
1 cup shredded white cheddar cheese
½ cup freshly grated Parmesan cheese
Mango-Chili Dipping Sauce

PREPARE QUESADILLAS
Preheat the oven to 400 degrees F. Use the roast or convection bake setting, if available.

Place 4 tortillas on a baking sheet. Spread 1 tablespoon of the goat cheese onto each tortilla. Follow with ⅜ cup of the Kalua Pork, ¼ cup of the cheddar and 2 tablespoons of the Parmesan, spreading each layer uniformly. Top each stack with another tortilla to form a sandwich, and compress lightly using the flat of your hand.

Bake quesadillas for 6 to 8 minutes, until cheese bubbles slightly and top of the tortillas are lightly browned. Use a wide spatula to lift each quesadilla onto a cutting board, and cut into 6 pieces.

ASSEMBLE
Place dipping sauce in a small bowl on a serving plate and arrange 6 quesadilla slices beside the sauce. Repeat for the remaining quesadillas.

Mango-Chili Dipping Sauce

MAKES ABOUT ¾ CUP

INGREDIENTS
1 mango
½ cup rice wine vinegar
2 tablespoons granulated sugar
1 clove garlic, minced (about 1 teaspoon)
1 tablespoon fresh cilantro leaves
1 teaspoon sambal oelek

PREPARATION
Peel mango and cut into ½-inch dice. Place half the chopped mango into a bowl, blender, or food processor and puree. Transfer mango puree to a small bowl. Place 2 tablespoons of the puree back into the blender. Add vinegar, sugar, garlic, cilantro and sambal. Blend with 3 short pulses, followed by 2 (3-second) pulses. Place in a bowl and add one-quarter of the chopped mango. (Use remaining puree mixed with remaining chopped mango as a sauce for ice cream, or mix it with your favorite plain yogurt for a snack.)

Kapulu Joes

In Hawaiian, kapulu means sloppy. We make them by mixing a tangy, slightly sweet and spicy sauce with some Kalua Pork (page 164). You could also use this sauce for barbecued chicken or even on burgers. I like to serve these sandwiches with Pineapple Cole Slaw (page 69). Be sure to provide lots of napkins as these puppies live up to their name.

MAKES ABOUT 2 CUPS SAUCE, ENOUGH FOR 8 SANDWICHES

INGREDIENTS

1 cup ketchup
½ cup brown sugar
1 teaspoon ground coriander
1½ teaspoons ground cumin
1½ teaspoons liquid smoke
⅓ cup rice wine vinegar
⅓ cup sweet chili sauce
1 teaspoon salt
¼ teaspoon freshly ground black pepper
Up to 2 pounds Kalua Pork (page 164)
Up to 8 bulkie rolls

PREPARATION

Combine ketchup, brown sugar, coriander, cumin, liquid smoke, vinegar, chili sauce, salt and pepper in a saucepan. Bring to a simmer over medium heat. Simmer, uncovered, for 10 minutes.

Mix Kalua Pork and sauce in a ratio of 1 pound pork to 1 cup sauce. Simmer until pork is heated through.

ASSEMBLE

While pork is heating, slice buns in half and toast. Place ¼ pound sauced pork onto each bun.

CHAPTER 6

Plantation Poultry Classics

A Room with a View

WHEN CHEF HANS-PETER HAGER called and offered me the Big Island job, I had only been back in the States for a few months. When I boarded that flight to Hawai'i, I had a duffel bag and $75 (and some would say not that much common sense). I called Chef Hager from the commuter terminal in Honolulu to tell him when I would be landing in Kona.

"Okay, Peeter, vee send somebody," he said.

"But how will they know who to look for?" I asked.

"Don't vorry about it," he said, and hung up.

To this day, landing at the Kona airport remains a thrill. I disembarked with 20 or so other passengers. Already disoriented by the six-hour time change, I tried to make sense of the jumbled lava rock terrain that stretched to the horizon, so different from the swaying palms and golden sand I had expected.

The Kailua Kona airport consisted of little more than a single thatched hut serving as the baggage claim area. I went to the curb and gazed out over the tiny, nearly empty parking lot. Right away I noticed a tall guy standing by an old Toyota station wagon. He looked at

me and said, "You must be the cook." I saw an open Heineken in his hand. I knew I was going to like this place.

T. Lowe, local driver and sous chef, drove us about 20 miles up the South Kohala coast on the one and only road, a two-lane highway that blasts through the lava fields and is still the only thoroughfare along this stretch of the island. Eventually, we turned into a row of tiny bungalows set on a secluded turquoise bay. Built by Laurence Rockefeller in 1965 to house the European cooks working at the Mauna Kea resort, they could not have been more perfectly picturesque for a mainlander with *Gilligan's Island* dreams. The other cooks welcomed me warmly and encouraged me to stay and take it easy as they headed off to start their shifts. I grabbed a beer from the refrigerator, went for a walk on the beach and ended up in the backyard hammock taking nap.

After a while, the cooks returned with the freshest fish imaginable. Twenty-four hours earlier I would never even have considered eating it raw, but that night I eagerly tasted the slices of 'ahi (tuna) dipped in shoyu (soy sauce). What a revelation! Then the cooks combined chunks of tuna and taco (octopus) with seaweed, spring onions and more shoyu to create my new favorite food—poke (pronounced poh-kee).

Several beers later, as a few of the cooks headed off to bed, I asked where my room was.

"So sorry, brah, you welcome to stay here, but we got no room or bed for you."

I didn't care. I happily pointed to the hammock on the beach and said, "It's okay. That'll be my room."

Chicken Papaya with Zinfandel

This recipe is a kind of homage to a Hawai'i tradition. Papaya is the source of the enzyme papain, which breaks down protein fibers, and therefore makes an effective meat tenderizer. Chicken papaya is traditionally made with green (unripe) papaya, which is higher in papain than the ripe fruit, probably because the star of the dish was often the tough loser of the cockfight! We substitute tender chicken breasts and fresh, ripe papaya to complement the rich wine sauce.

SERVES 4

CHICKEN
4 (5-ounce) boneless chicken breasts, skinless or skin on
1 tablespoon salt
2 teaspoons freshly ground black pepper
¼ cup vegetable oil

SAUCE
¼ cup shallots, chopped
1 cup Zinfandel wine
1 teaspoon cornstarch dissolved in ¼-cup cold water
¼ cup cold, unsalted butter
½ papaya, peeled, seeded and cut into ¼-inch dice

PREPARE CHICKEN
Heat a large sauté pan on high for 1 minute. As it heats, season both sides of each chicken breast with salt and pepper. Add oil to the hot pan, swirling gently to coat, and place chicken in the pan, skin side down. (If the breasts are skinless, the "skin" side is the smoother side.) Cook for 4 to 5 minutes, and turn; the chicken should be golden to dark brown in color and release easily from the pan. Cook 4 to 8 minutes more, until the thickest part of the breast reads at least 160 degrees F using an instant-read thermometer. (Cooking time will depend on the size and thickness of each piece.)

PREPARE SAUCE
Transfer chicken to a platter and cover with foil to keep warm. Add shallots to the pan, reduce heat to medium-high and cook for 1 to 2 minutes, stirring continuously, until transparent. Add wine, stirring to deglaze the pan, and boil until only ¼ cup remains. Stir in cornstarch mixture and bring sauce back to a boil. Whisk in butter and immediately turn off heat.

ASSEMBLE
Place raw papaya atop each chicken breast, and spoon sauce over chicken and fruit.

Chicken Shoyu

Shoyu is how we say soy sauce in Hawai'i. This dish features the salty sauce, paired with its best friends—ginger and garlic—and sweetened with brown sugar. The surprise is the citrus flavoring. In Hawai'i, chicken shoyu is always made with thighs, which are the flavorful part of the chicken. If you feel you must use breasts, please use bone-in breasts with the skin on. A boneless, skinless breast will dry out in this cooking method. Here in Hawai'i, chicken shoyu is be served with rice, but I sometimes serve mine with egg noodles.

SERVES 6 TO 8

INGREDIENTS

1 lemon

1 orange

1 cup soy sauce

1¼ cups water

½ cup brown sugar

1 (2-inch) piece fresh ginger root,
    peeled and minced (about 2 tablespoons)

2 cloves garlic, thinly sliced

8 chicken thighs, bone-in and skin on

½ cup cornstarch

3 tablespoons vegetable oil, divided

1 tablespoon sriracha

½ cup scallions, green parts only,
    cut into ½-inch lengths

1 tablespoon sesame seeds,
    lightly toasted in a dry skillet

PREPARE CHICKEN

Preheat oven to 375 degrees F.

Zest the lemon and orange. Juice the lemon and half of the orange; set juice aside. Place lemon zest and half of the orange zest in a bowl. Add soy sauce, water, brown sugar, ginger and garlic. Whisk to combine and dissolve sugar. Add chicken to the mixture and press to submerge. Cover and refrigerate for 2 to 6 hours.

Remove chicken to a plate, allowing excess sauce to drain. Reserve marinade. Spread cornstarch on a flat plate. Press chicken into the cornstarch, coating both sides, starting with the skin side. Hold coated chicken over the plate and pat to remove excess cornstarch.

Heat a heavy roasting pan or ovensafe skillet on high for 1 minute. Add 1½ tablespoons of the vegetable oil and add half the chicken, skin side down. Lightly brown both sides of the chicken and transfer to a clean plate. Repeat with remaining 1½ tablespoons of the oil and remaining chicken. Return all chicken to the pan and carefully (it may splatter) add reserved marinade, but not to cover; the chicken skin should be visible. Place the pan, uncovered, in the oven and bake about 35 to 40 minutes, until the largest thigh reaches 165 degrees F using an instant-read thermometer. Place chicken on a platter and sprinkle with the remaining orange zest. Add sriracha and lemon and orange juices to the sauce. Pour sauce over chicken and garnish with scallions and sesame seeds.

Merriman's Kapalua, Maui

Tane Datta—Adaptations

TANE DATTA NEVER PLANNED to be a farmer. In the early 1970s, he got interested in back-to-the-land ideas, environmental protection and self-sufficiency. He wasn't thinking about farming, he was thinking about alternative energy and getting off the grid. Then he saw how farming connected humans to the natural environment, and he started looking for some land.

He also ended up in Hawai'i by chance. In 1979, he was preparing to move to Weaverville, California, when his mother offered him the use of a free companion ticket to visit the islands. One look at the lush vegetation and incredible microclimates, and he was changing his plans. After exploring Maui and Kaua'i, he settled near Kealakekua on the Big Island of Hawai'i.

In the months prior to opening The Gallery restaurant, I was living in sunny, arid Puako on the South Kohala coast. Tane was living about an hour away, in rainy, tropical Kealakekua. Tane had built a solar food dryer in Puako at Chef Sandy Barr's house and made the drive every week to check on it, which is how he happened to be at a neighborhood potluck one night that I also attended.

Tane remembers the excitement of our early conversations. "We were both in the early concept stage," he says, "and both very optimistic. I didn't care about making a lot of money. I just wanted to make enough to keep farming, and to help others keep farming." That worked for me, because what I wanted was to serve high-quality, locally grown food. As Tane says, "We were each other's solution waiting to happen."

From an economic perspective, Tane is primarily driven by two factors: the highest sustainable value of the land, meaning the right crop to make enough money to live on while still protecting the soil, and creating opportunities for small farmers to succeed. "Plus, it's fun—the constant exploration, looking for new crops," he says. In the beginning, he worked with just four other farmers. Now his Adaptations company distributes for about 100 farmers every year. Recently he's also helped develop a microloan program, Hawai'i Island Food Producers Fund, supported through local donations and crowd sourcing to equalize access to capital for small farmers.

On a deeper level, Tane says he hopes that his food helps reconnect people with nature. "Not everybody can grow their food, but just eating well-grown food is a way of connecting to the earth."

Not-the-Usual Cashew Chicken (It's all about that prep!)

Like most stir-fry dishes, it's all in the prep for this cashew chicken. In the restaurant kitchen, each cook lays out the ingredients for whatever dishes he or she is responsible for. The French phrase for this is mise en place, which means put in place. Use small dishes (even paper plates will work) for each of your measured ingredients so they are at your fingertips before you start heating the pan. When the pan is hot, add the oil and keep moving. In less than 10 minutes it will be ready to serve. Don't forget to make some white or brown rice ahead of time.

SERVES 4 TO 6

MARINATED CUCUMBER

½ *cucumber, halved lengthwise, peeled, seeded and sliced into ¼-inch pieces (about 1 cup)*
1 *tablespoon sherry vinegar or rice wine vinegar*

CHICKEN

1½ *pounds boneless, skinless chicken breast, cut into ½ x 3-inch strips*
2 *tablespoons vegetable oil*

STIR-FRY

2 *tablespoons vegetable oil, divided*
4 *carrots, sliced ¼-inch thick (about 1 cup)*
4 *stalks celery, sliced ½-inch thick (about 1 cup)*
1 *small onion, chopped (about 1 cup)*
8 *white or cremini mushrooms, quartered*
2 *large cloves garlic, minced*
1 *(3-inch) piece fresh ginger root, peeled and minced (about 3 tablespoons)*
½ *cup apple juice*
¾ *cup soy sauce*
1 *cup whole roasted, unsalted cashews*
2 *teaspoons sambal oelek*
½ *cup dry sherry*
1 *cup fresh pineapple, cut into ¼-inch cubes*
½ *cup fresh cilantro, chopped*
White or brown rice

PREPARE MARINATED CUCUMBER

Toss sliced cucumber with vinegar and set aside.

PREPARE CHICKEN

Heat a large skillet or wok on high heat for 3 minutes. While pan is heating, blot chicken with paper towels (for better browning). Add the oil to the pan and add chicken. Stir-fry until seared on all sides and remove to a plate.

PREPARE STIR-FRY

Still on high heat, add 1 tablespoon of the oil to the pan, and add carrots, celery and onion. Stir-fry for 2 to 3 minutes until onions are softened. Push vegetables to the periphery of the pan, add remaining 1 tablespoon of the oil to the center and add mushrooms, garlic and ginger. Combine with vegetables and stir-fry for 1 minute. Add apple juice and continue stir-frying on high until juice just starts to boil. Reduce heat to medium and add cooked chicken, soy sauce, cashews and sambal oelek, stirring and tossing to combine. Add sherry and pineapple. Stir to combine and turn off the heat. Add cilantro and toss well.

ASSEMBLE

Serve cashew chicken over rice and top with marinated cucumber slices.

Mr. Big Shot—Not

ONE OF MY FAVORITE Hawaiian/pidgin words is kolohe (kow-low-hey), in English we say rascal. Folks in Hawai'i will talk about "some bugga is kolohe" and not be passing judgment on that person. They're simply telling the truth. Folks here tend to treat everyone as equals. For those of us who are overweight, this can be unsettling. When a friend I hadn't seen in years called to tell me she saw me on TV, "And you looked good." "Yeah," she added, "you come thick, too." How I love the people in Hawai'i.

When Merriman's Waimea had been open for a few years, we were in *The New York Times* and other large publications, and starting to gain some attention. One afternoon while we were closed between lunch and dinner, I found myself alone in the dining room as JT Dupoit walked in. I hadn't seen JT since I'd left the hotel. He was one of those lovable kolohe buggas working in the dish room. JT walked in under the giant Merriman's sign hanging over the front entrance and past the framed copy of the *Los Angeles Times* article about me and the restaurant. JT was surprised to see me in my chef whites.

He said, "Howzit Pete, you working here?"

"Yes," I replied.

"How long you been working here?" he asked.

"Since it opened," I responded.

"How is it?"

"It's great!"

That's Hawai'i.

That's how I knew how much of a big shot I was.

Monkeypod Kitchen by Merriman, Wailea, Maui

Hiring at the Beach— The Glamorous Life of a Chef

WHEN I MOVED TO THE BIG ISLAND in 1983, I did so as a cook, to help open the Mauna Lani Bay Hotel. This was only the third hotel to open on the Kohala coast. In 1989, shortly after I opened Merriman's, the Hyatt Regency opened with 1,290 rooms, more than doubling the number of hotel rooms on Kohala's sparsely populated coast.

Hiring became an almost herculean task. A person could walk into Merriman's to ask for an application and be on the floor, in uniform, 15 minutes later! Busboys became rock stars. Dishwashers were just about impossible to find. We tried every trick in the guerrilla-guide-to-hiring handbook. For example, stop for every hitchhiker and offer a job, or call the local pastor to ask about folks down on their luck.

Exacerbating the workforce situation was our inconsistent demand. We were a new restaurant and might do 40 covers one night and 140 the next. Sure enough, one afternoon, I was looking at 140 reservations, and we had no dishwasher. Reaching deep into my bag of hiring tricks, I drove to the "hippie beach" near Puako. I thought surely one of the folks living on the beach could use some cash from an evening of dishwashing. I was about mid-interview with this long-haired beach dweller when it struck me: *Dude, you are interviewing a naked man!*

We closed the deal—he would wash dishes that night for $60 cash and a six-pack. Oh, and I did insist he show up fully clothed.

Hawai'i-Style Jerk Chicken

While driving around the main Hawaiian islands, you might notice roadside vendors offering pateles, which are Puerto Rican tamales made with grated green banana. Too much work to include in this cookbook, but I mention them because they are part of another legacy that has contributed to Hawaiian cuisine. Caribbean influence on Hawaiian culture dates back to 1900, when the first Puerto Ricans arrived to work the sugar plantations. The mixture of spices and sugar to season meats probably arrived with those folks. If you enjoy very spicy food, finely chop a Hawaiian chili pepper and add it to the rub. A bird's eye or Thai chili will suffice.

SERVES 6

CHICKEN

2 tablespoons dark brown sugar

1 tablespoon coarse salt

½ tablespoon ground cardamom

1 tablespoon ground cumin

½ tablespoon cayenne pepper

½ tablespoon ground coriander

1 tablespoon ground cinnamon

6 boneless, skinless chicken breasts

1 ½ tablespoons vegetable oil, divided

PREPARE CHICKEN

Preheat the oven to 350 degrees F.

Mix brown sugar, salt, cardamom, cumin, cayenne pepper, coriander, and cinnamon in a small bowl. Rub each chicken breast with ½ teaspoon of the vegetable oil and 1 tablespoon of the spice mixture to form a light crust.

Heat the remaining tablespoon of oil on high heat in a heavy-bottomed, ovenproof skillet. Add chicken and cook for about 2 minutes on each side until brown and crusty. (Brown in batches, if chicken breasts are large.) When all the chicken is browned, place the skillet in the oven and cook until breasts reach 160 degrees F on an instant-read thermometer, about 15 to 20 minutes, depending on size.

This chicken is delicious with Pineapple-Mint Chutney (page 143) or Pineapple Cole Slaw (page 69). You can also slice the cooked breasts and serve them on a crunchy green salad.

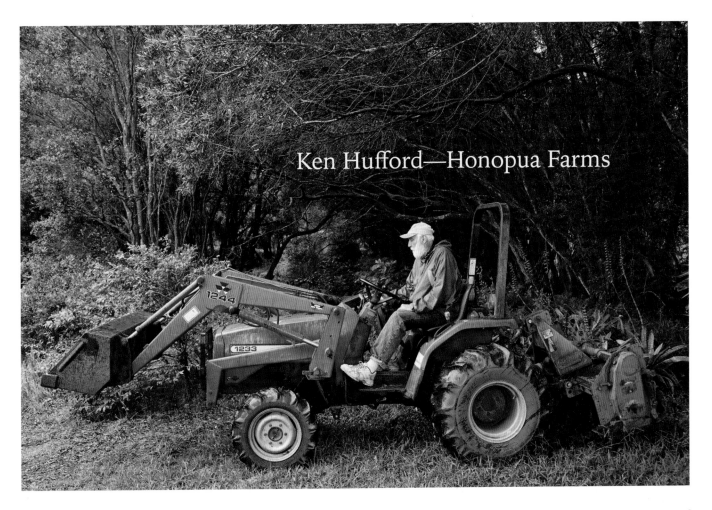

Ken Hufford—Honopua Farms

KEN HUFFORD AND HIS WIFE ROEN grow a wonderful assortment of organic vegetables on ten acres in Waimea. What makes their farm really special is the smell of fresh lavender in the air. Roen's parents, Marie and Bill McDonald, started growing flowers and lavender over 30 years ago, and Marie, who is well known for making leis, wrote about the art of lei-making in *Ka Lei: The Leis of Hawaii*, with illustrations by Roen.

In the mid-1990s, when Marie and Bill retired, Ken and Roen discovered that the Waimea climate was perfect for growing a wide variety of crops—kale, lettuces, carrots, beets, turnips and cabbage. Today, Ken concentrates on the vegetables, while Roen continues to grow the lavender along with protea and other flowers.

When Merriman's started farm-to-fork tours, Honopua Farms was at the top of the list of local growers to visit. I knew Ken and Roen would be wonderful ambassadors for "farming with aloha."

Roast Chicken with Preserved Lemon—Hula Grill Maui

In this recipe, first make the preserved lemons for the salsa, and then use the lemon-flavored water as part of the brine for the chicken. Even just one hour of brining really helps keep the chicken moist, especially since it cooks for less than an hour at a high temperature. I like to serve this chicken with mashed potatoes and Roasted Brussels Sprouts (page 92).

SERVES 4 TO 6

PRESERVE LEMONS AND BRINED CHICKEN

4 quarts water, divided

¾ cup table salt, divided

¼ cup sugar

1 (2½-inch) piece fresh ginger root,
    peeled and cut into 5 (½-inch) pieces

2 bay leaves

2 lemons, quartered

1 (3½–4 pound) whole roasting chicken

PREPARE LEMONS

Place 2 quarts of the water, ¼ cup of the salt, sugar, ginger and bay leaves into a 4-quart saucepan. Bring to a boil, stirring occasionally to dissolve salt and sugar. Boil for 1 minute. Add lemons. Reduce heat to simmer and cook, uncovered, for 20 minutes or until rinds are soft. Remove lemons to a cutting board or plate to cool. Reserve liquid.

BRINE CHICKEN

In a pot large enough to submerge chicken, place 2 quarts cold water, remaining ½ cup of the salt and leftover lemon cooking liquid. Stir to dissolve salt. Cool brine in the refrigerator for 30 minutes. Submerge chicken in brine and refrigerate for 1 to 3 hours. If the pot is too large for your fridge, reduce water and add ice to the brine to keep it cool.

PRESERVED LEMONS SALSA

¼ *cup fresh cilantro, roughly chopped*

1 tomato, chopped into ¼-inch dice (about 1 cup)

1 clove garlic, minced

2 tablespoons finely chopped Preserved Lemons

2 teaspoons freshly grated ginger root

½ *teaspoon salt*

½ *teaspoon freshly ground black pepper*

1 tablespoon rice wine vinegar

¼ *cup olive oil*

PREPARE SALSA

Gently toss cilantro, tomato, garlic, preserved lemon and ginger in a small bowl. Add salt, pepper, vinegar and olive oil. Mix well.

ROAST CHICKEN

Brined Chicken

2 teaspoons salt, divided

½ *teaspoon freshly ground black pepper, divided*

PREPARE CHICKEN

Preheat the oven to 475 degrees F.

Remove chicken from brine, and thoroughly pat dry (inside and out) with paper towels. Place chicken, breast side down, in a roasting pan. Season the back with 1 teaspoon of the salt and ¼ teaspoon of the pepper. Place in the center of the oven and roast for 15 minutes. The back skin should be nicely browned.

Turn chicken breast side up. Season with the remaining salt and pepper. Continue roasting until breast begins to brown, about 10 minutes. Reduce heat to 375 degrees F and cook 10 minutes more. Using an instant-read thermometer, check temperature in the thickest part of the thigh; the chicken is done when it reaches 160 degrees F. Cook 5 to 10 minutes longer, if needed.

ASSEMBLE

Place chicken on a cutting board and let rest for 5 minutes. Carve chicken and place meat on a platter. Dot arranged meat with Preserved Lemon Salsa. Pass remaining salsa at the table.

CHAPTER 7

Cooking Like a Local

Doi's Store

IN 1983, the heart of Kawaihae and the entire South Kohala coast, was the T. Doi & Sons Store. Kawaihae was a very remote spot until the Queen Ka'ahumanu highway was completed in 1975, and even in 1983 the population was only about 75. But it had the islands' second deep-water port after Hilo, and that's a big deal in a place that relies so much on imports and exports. The first cattle in Hawai'i were brought to shore in Kawaihae by Captain George Vancouver in 1793, and it remains a cattle-shipping port to this day. During the Big Island's

sugar plantation era, tons of raw sugar left Kawaihae bound for the US mainland.

The Doi family operated the general store and gas station in this tiny, arid port town. Mr. Doi pumped gas and did outboard engine repair. Mrs. Doi and her sister ran the general store, selling more items than a Walmart and Home Depot combined—fresh vegetables, sushi, camping gear, tools, clothing, bamboo fishing pools, beer, medicines of all types and much more—and Mrs. Doi could always find whatever you needed in about two seconds.

The Dois were perhaps the most ingenious marketers and business operators I have ever seen. To encourage folks to make the treacherous ten-mile trip down the mountain from Waimea and beyond, the Dois kept a menagerie with monkeys and exotic birds.

(By the time I started to frequent the store in 1983, their little zoo had closed, but the cages were still out back.) The store also featured one of the first televisions on the Big Island. As a loss leader, they sold fresh fish sandwiches for $1—white bread, iceberg lettuce, sliced tomato and super-fresh fish cooked to order—now that's something you can get a hankering for! After every practice at the canoe club, I'd race my fellow paddlers to be the first to put in my sandwich order.

Mrs. Doi was more than a fantastic business operator who could daily attract at least half the village population for a fish sandwich. She also embodied the caring community spirit that is Hawai'i—the spirit of aloha. In 1984, I had back surgery and spent a couple of months confined to the floor of our bungalow in Puako. My friend Brian stopped by on his way to Doi's store, and I asked him to pick up a head of lettuce for me. He returned without the lettuce, they were all out. He helped me outdoors to the floor of the lana'i and stayed to "talk story" for a bit. About an hour later, a car pulled into the driveway. "You Pete Merriman?" the driver asked. "Yes," I replied. He got out of the car, walked up to the lana'i and handed me a head of lettuce. "Mrs. Doi said you wanted this," he said. I took the lettuce and he headed back to the car as I yelled "Mahalo!"

That's why we say, *Lucky live Hawai'i!*

Bean Thread Noodles and Sweet Chili Shrimp

Bean thread noodles are long, thin, translucent noodles made from mung bean starch. In Hawai'i they are known as long rice. Lighter and more fragile than wheat or rice noodles, of course they are gluten-free. This dish should be served cold or at room temperature—perfect for an outdoor picnic or potluck.

SERVES 4

INGREDIENTS

12 colossal shrimp (U-8) peeled and deveined

1 tablespoon plus 2 teaspoons kosher salt

2 (4-ounce) packages bean thread noodles

3 tablespoons toasted sesame oil

¾ cup bottled sweet chili sauce

½ cucumber, halved lengthwise, peeled, seeded and sliced into ¼-inch pieces

3 ounces snow peas or sugar snap peas, diagonally cut in half

¼ cup red onion or scallion, thinly sliced

¼ cup carrot, julienned

½ cup fresh cilantro leaves

½ cup roasted, unsalted macadamia nuts, roughly chopped

PREPARE SHRIMP

Add shrimp to 2 quarts boiling water, add I tablespoon salt and cook for 2 minutes or until pink. Cool, peel, and cut each shrimp into 3 or 4 pieces.

PREPARE LONG RICE

Place noodles in a large bowl and add enough boiling water to cover. Let sit for 15 minutes; drain and rinse with cold water. (If you like, using clean scissors, cut noodles into shorter lengths for easier serving and eating.)

ASSEMBLE

Add sesame oil and remaining salt to the drained noodles and toss. Add sweet chili sauce and toss until well coated. Add cucumber, peas, onion, carrots, and shrimp and toss. Divide among 4 large bowls and top with cilantro and macadamia nuts.

Cucumber Namasu

This is a refreshing and crunchy, sweet-and-sour side dish or garnish. Daikon is a large white, mild radish popular in Japan. If you can only get waxed cucumbers, submerge them in a one-to-one mixture of white vinegar and water for 2 minutes, then rub with a kitchen towel to remove the loosened wax, and rinse under cool water; or just peel them. Everything should be sliced thin, to about ⅛ inch. If you have a mandoline, this is a great time to use it.

MAKES ABOUT 4 CUPS

INGREDIENTS

1½ cups rice wine vinegar

1 cup sugar

½ tablespoon table salt

1 large English cucumber, thinly sliced,
    or 2 unwaxed cucumbers,
    halved, seeded and thinly sliced

½ red onion, thinly sliced

¼ daikon (about 6 x 2 inches) peeled,
    halved lengthwise and thinly sliced

1 large carrot, thinly sliced on the diagonal

PREPARATION

Combine vinegar, sugar, and salt in a stainless steel pan and heat on low, stirring, just until salt and sugar are dissolved. Remove from the heat and let cool. Place sliced cucumber, onion, daikon and carrot in a large bowl. Pour vinegar mixture over vegetables, toss, and refrigerate for at least 2 hours before serving. The cucumbers will release additional liquid, so serve using a slotted spoon or tongs.

Kurt Hirabara—Hirabara Farms

ON A FARM of less than three acres, Kurt Hirabara and his wife, Pam, produce amazing quantities of specialty lettuces and herbs. "I've always had a knack for getting high volume out of small spaces," Kurt told me, "I kind of go against the popular beliefs about growing, and somehow it works for me." What turned me on to Hirabara Farms, though, was the variety and exceptional quality of their salad greens. Kurt says staying small helps maintain quality because he can control every aspect of the growing process.

Kurt has a degree in horticulture and says he is naturally inclined toward experimentation. His first career was with a research company on O'ahu, helping develop an organic recycling program using cattle waste. During down time, the company asked him to "grow something" in the greenhouses on the property. Kurt did a little research and, through a friend, discovered a winter market for fresh, US-grown herbs in Los Angeles. The herbs were so impressive that one of the LA farm owners asked Kurt to consult on his mesclun growing practices in Southern California. And that's when Kurt started thinking about growing baby lettuces in Hawai'i. "The waste recycling program stalled, and I started to see that maybe my future was as a scientist-farmer rather than a pure scientist," he told me.

In 1993, Kurt and Pam moved to the Big Island and started farming on land about 11 miles outside of Hilo. The next year he attended a fundraiser that featured the Hawai'i Regional Cuisine chefs. Kurt's plan was to work with just one of them, Chef Philippe Padovani, to perfect his lettuces. "I figured if I could meet the standards of one of these demanding chefs, I'd have a product they would

all want," he says. It took almost six months before Chef Padovani declared the lettuce "perfect" and started referring other chefs to Hirabara Farms.

After only three years, Kurt and Pam's farm was threatened by vog—the acid-laden volcanic haze that builds up when emissions from Kilauea react with oxygen, water vapor, and sunlight—blown into the Hilo area by an unusual pattern of winds. They decided to move, and after an extensive search for a new site, they settled on Waimea—a great addition to the Merriman's "neighborhood."

We have been serving their produce, including red oak, frisée, cocarde, and lollo rossa lettuces, for over 15 years. Their dedication to consistent quality makes it possible for us to give diners a really memorable salad.

Kurt and Pam are the perfect team—he is the left-brain scientist who reads the research and loves to test new lettuce varieties, while she is the right-brain creative one who does the marketing and asks just the right questions to keep the business on the cutting edge.

When we talked, Kurt complimented me on "walking the talk"—because my commitment to the farmers has not wavered. That's high praise, considering the source, and I couldn't do it without farmers like Pam and Kurt Hirabara.

Warm Spinach Salad with Pipikaula

This salad is all about the dressing. We start with a fairly classic warm bacon dressing, sweeten it with a little honey and then, to make it really special, we add some chopped pipikaula. The salad itself is simple—spinach, sweet onion and grapefruit to add some tang. The perfect forkful includes a little of every ingredient. Enjoy it as an appetizer or a meal.

SERVES 4 AS AN APPETIZER OR SERVES 2 AS A MAIN COURSE

INGREDIENTS

8 ounces fresh spinach, stemmed

¼ cup sweet onion, diced

Grapefruit supremes cut from 1 grapefruit

4 slices bacon, cut into ¼-inch strips

1 shallot, thinly sliced

3 tablespoons Dijon mustard

3 tablespoons honey

⅓ cup balsamic vinegar

¼ cup olive oil

½ teaspoon table salt

½ teaspoon freshly ground black pepper

¼ cup diced Pipikaula (page 149)

2 tablespoons freshly squeezed lemon juice

PREPARE SALAD AND DRESSING

Place spinach, onion and grapefruit supremes in a salad bowl.

Preheat a sauté pan to medium-high, add bacon pieces and cook until just barely crispy. Stir in shallots and sauté until softened, about 1 minute. Stir in Dijon mustard, follow with honey and stir. Stir in balsamic vinegar and scrape the bottom of the pan to deglaze. Gradually whisk in oil. Remove from heat and add salt and pepper. Add Pipikaula and lemon juice, stirring to combine.

ASSEMBLE

If Pipikaula and lemon juice were previously refrigerated, gently reheat dressing until hot enough to wilt spinach. Pour over salad, toss and serve.

Macadamia Nut Pesto

Traditional pesto is made with pine nuts, but here in the islands, we've got macadamia nuts literally growing on trees. They have the same buttery texture as pine nuts, but they're much richer and fuller, so much so that we leave out the Parmesan cheese. The result is a pesto that seems fresher and lighter on pasta or mixed into rice. Try a small dollop on grilled swordfish or mahi-mahi, or use it to spice up broiled or baked chicken breast. Cook the chicken until just done, then spread $\frac{1}{8}$ inch of the pesto on top and place chicken under the broiler until a nice crust forms. *Note:* If you cannot find unsalted macadamia nuts, use salted nuts and omit kosher salt.

MAKES 1¼ CUPS

PESTO

1 cup fresh basil leaves, loosely packed
⅓ cup fresh flat-leaf parsley leaves, loosely packed
⅔ cup roasted, unsalted macadamia nuts,
    coarsely chopped
4 medium cloves garlic, trimmed
1½ teaspoons kosher salt plus extra, to taste
½ teaspoon red pepper flakes
¾ cup extra-virgin olive oil

PREPARE PESTO

After washing, thoroughly dry the basil and parsley. Place basil, parsley, macadamia nuts, garlic, salt and red pepper flakes into a blender or small food processor, and blend using 8 to 10 pulses, then pulse continuously for 15 seconds. With the blender running, add olive oil in a slow, steady stream until mixture resembles a smooth paste. Add salt, if desired.

Kawaihae Canoe Club

Monkeypod Kitchen Saimin

Raise your hand if you've ever had ramen noodles from a packet. Saimin is Hawaiʻi's version of ramen that was inspired by noodle soups from Japan, China and the Philippines. It's easy to make, versatile—you can add or substitute your own favorite ingredients—and so comforting. At Monkeypod, we like to use Kalua Pork (page 164), but you can use another protein (even Spam, another Hawaiian favorite) or tofu or just more vegetables. Be sure to slurp your noodles!

SERVES 4

BROTH
2 cups boiling water plus extra, as needed
1 teaspoon granulated dashi
3 tablespoons soy sauce
2 cups chicken or vegetable broth

NOODLES
16 ounces saimin noodles
(any long, thin wheat noodle, such as ramen or vermicelli)

VEGETABLES
1 crown broccoli, florets only, cut into bite-size pieces
4 ounces green beans, cut into bite-size pieces

FOR ASSEMBLY
4 cups Saimin Broth
1 pound Kalua Pork (page 164)
1 cup bean sprouts
1 red onion, thinly sliced
½ cup roasted, unsalted peanuts
8 sprigs fresh cilantro
¼ cup fresh mint leaves

PREPARE SAIMIN BROTH
Combine boiling water, dashi and soy sauce in a pot. Bring to a simmer, add broth and return to a simmer. Taste for saltiness, adding more water, if needed. (Dashi is very salty and different brands may vary, so season it the way you like it.) Cover and keep hot.

PREPARE NOODLES AND VEGETABLES
Bring a large pot of water to a boil and add noodles. Cook according to package directions until al dente. Without draining the pot, remove noodles using a strainer and divide among 4 large, deep bowls. Immediately add broccoli and green beans to the boiling water and cook for about 3 minutes. Using a strainer, remove cooked vegetables and divide among 4 bowls with noodles.

ASSEMBLE
Pour 1 cup hot Saimin Broth into each of the bowls. Add equal portions of pork, sprouts, onion, peanuts, cilantro and mint to each bowl.

Three Pillars
of Peter's Palate

AT MERRIMAN'S we feature the freshest and best-quality ingredients available. Then we complement these foods with simple but bold marinades, sauces or salsas, often based on the three pillars of flavor—garlic, ginger and shoyu (soy sauce)—originating out of the many cultures of Hawai'i.

Vegan Portuguese Bean Soup

This is a very popular soup throughout the islands, and every cook has his or her favorite recipe. I like to add wheat pasta or egg noodles to this soup, or maybe some kale. If you don't have liquid smoke, replace the 2 tablespoons paprika with 1 tablespoon smoked paprika plus 1 tablespoon sweet paprika.

MAKES 2 QUARTS

SOUP

2 tablespoons olive oil

2 medium onions, chopped

1 small leek, white part only, halved lengthwise
    and sliced into ¼-inch pieces

4 medium carrots, cut into ½-inch dice

2 large stalks celery, cut into ½-inch slices

4 medium cloves garlic, finely chopped

1 dried bay leaf

2 tablespoons paprika

1 tablespoon ground cumin

½ teaspoon ground coriander

1 tablespoon table salt plus extra, to taste

¼ teaspoon liquid smoke

4 cups water

1 can (14.5–16 ounces) diced tomatoes

1 can (14.5–16 ounces) kidney beans,
    drained and rinsed

3 tablespoons sherry vinegar

Freshly ground black pepper

¼ cup fresh parsley, chopped

PREPARE SOUP

In a 4-quart pot over medium heat, heat olive oil for 30 seconds. Add onion, leek, carrot, celery and garlic. Cook 5 to 7 minutes, stirring occasionally, until vegetables are slightly softened. Add bay leaf, paprika, cumin, coriander, salt, liquid smoke, water, tomatoes and beans. Stir to mix well. Turn the heat to high and bring soup just to a boil. Partially cover the pot and reduce heat to medium-low, adjusting as necessary, for a slow simmer. Simmer, partially covered, for 30 minutes. Add vinegar. Increase the heat to high and bring to a boil. Cook at a low boil for 2 minutes more. Add salt and pepper, if desired.

ASSEMBLE

Ladle into serving bowls and garnish with fresh parsley.

Watercress Kimchi

Kimchi is so versatile—put it on a sandwich, serve it with any smoked meat or any unsmoked meat for that matter, and mix it into eggs or rice or a little of both. Usually it's made with cabbage, but I use watercress because that's how Mrs. Kim made it for me when I was the banquet chef at the Mauna Lani. With the soft cress, the kimchi cures in 12 to 24 hours. Keep some around all the time.

MAKES 10 TO 12 SERVINGS

INGREDIENTS

1 (4-ounce) bunch watercress
4 tablespoons kosher salt, divided
2 cups water
1 cup rice wine vinegar
3 tablespoons sambal oelek
1 tablespoon nuoc mam or nam pla
1 teaspoon granulated sugar
1 onion, quartered and thinly sliced
1 carrot, cut into 1-inch julienned strips
1 red bell pepper, cut into 1-inch julienned strips
4 cloves garlic, thinly sliced

PREPARATION

Cut watercress stems from leaves. Cut stems into 1-inch pieces and reserve leaves. In a bowl, dissolve 3 tablespoons of the salt in water. Soak watercress stems in salted water for 15 minutes. Drain, but do not rinse the stems.

Place vinegar, sambal, nuoc mam, sugar and remaining tablespoon of the salt in a large bowl, and stir to dissolve sugar and salt. Add watercress stems and leaves, onion, carrot, bell pepper and garlic. Mix well. Cover and refrigerate overnight.

Above, from left to right: Kalani Graciidis,
Mark Sadang and Kekoa Kabalis.
Opposite, clockwise from left to right:
Kalani Graciidis, Chantel Lorenzo-Beaudet,
Taira Cran, Lizzie Harris, Kekoa Kabalis,
Mark Sadang, Amalyn Raymond, and
Peter Merriman at the Kawaihae Canoe Club.

CHAPTER 8

The Sweet Life

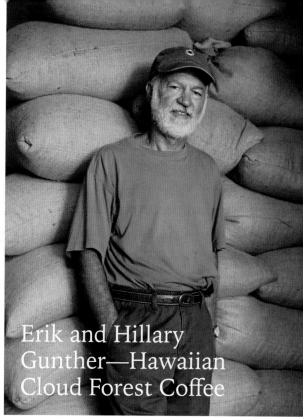

Erik and Hillary Gunther—Hawaiian Cloud Forest Coffee

ON A PHOTO SHOOT for this cookbook, I was reminded of the many things that make up-country Hawai'i so special. We were running a few minutes behind schedule and could not make the customary stop at Tex Drive-In in Honokea. Reputed to have the best malasadas in the Hawaiian Islands, it's worth a stop whenever I happen to be passing.

Instead, we turned mauka (toward the mountain) to visit Erik and Hillary Gunther at their coffee farm, known as Hawaiian Cloud Forest Coffee. The Gunthers grow and roast one of the best tasting coffees in the world.

Their farm is beautiful, lush and immaculate. A visit alone to the volcanic slopes of Mauna Kea counts as a special day. Add to that the opportunity to drink the world's best coffee for a photo with our delightful hosts, and we know we're fortunate.

Erik and Hillary have been eating at Merriman's since we first opened in 1988. They're emblematic of all of Hawai'i's farmers—gracious, humble and intelligent. They not only produce great crops, but are careful stewards of the land.

Merriman's Signature Chocolate Purse

This dessert is my daughter Jessie's favorite. She orders it whenever we visit one of the Merriman's restaurants. The crunchy phyllo adds just the right amount of texture, and who doesn't love chocolate with vanilla ice cream? In some of the restaurants, we serve the purse in a pool of caramel sauce. At home, I usually skip the sauce. The recipe takes a little planning, but you can prepare the purses ahead of time and quickly bake them just before serving. Your family and guests will thank you.

MAKES 12 PURSES

CHOCOLATE FILLING
8 ounces chocolate (70% cacao),
  chopped into ½-inch pieces
2 ounces chocolate (55% cacao),
  chopped into ½-inch pieces
⅜ cup water
1 tablespoon instant coffee
  dissolved in 2 tablespoons boiling water
1 cup granulated sugar
4 eggs
12 tablespoons (1½ sticks) unsalted butter,
  softened, plus extra for greasing
1 tablespoon all-purpose flour

FOR ASSEMBLY
8 tablespoons clarified butter (page 116), melted
8 tablespoons cocoa powder
6 (8 x 16-inch) sheets phyllo dough
12 teaspoons granulated sugar
Vanilla ice cream

PREPARE FILLING
Preheat the oven to 300 degrees F.

Place all chopped chocolate in a large bowl. Measure water, coffee and ¼ cup of the sugar into a small saucepan and bring to a boil over medium-high heat. Pour boiling mixture over the chocolate and stir until the chocolate melts. In a separate bowl, whisk eggs until the whites and yolks are well combined. Add remaining ¾ cup of the sugar and continue to whisk until pale yellow in color. Set aside.

Whisk softened butter into melted chocolate mixture until well combined. Whisk in egg-sugar mixture. Sprinkle in flour and whisk to combine.

Grease an 8 x 8-inch baking pan with butter or vegetable shortening, add chocolate mixture and place inside a larger baking pan. Add warm water to the larger pan until halfway up the sides of the smaller pan. Place on the middle rack of the preheated oven and bake for 30 minutes. The filling can be prepared up to a day ahead of serving. If preparing ahead, cover and store in the refrigerator.

ASSEMBLE PURSES
Preheat the oven to 400 degrees F.

Using a knife, divide the filling (which should be the consistency of a firm pudding) into 12 equal portions. In a small bowl, whisk melted clarified butter and cocoa together to form a slurry. Remove phyllo from package, keeping the sheets rolled up, and cover with a damp towel. Working quickly to avoid drying, unroll 1 phyllo sheet and, using a pastry brush, paint with butter-cocoa slurry and sprinkle with 1 teaspoon of the sugar. Fold phyllo sheet in half so the longest edges meet, and press to adhere. Paint the top layer with butter-cocoa slurry. Cut the phyllo in half crosswise to form 2 equal rectangles and place 1 portion of the chocolate filling in the center of each rectangle. Working with each rectangle separately, gather up the edges of the phyllo and press together to form the purse. Place both purses on a baking sheet and repeat to make 12 purses total. If not baking immediately, cover in plastic wrap and store in a cool place for up to 2 hours.

Bake purses for 3 to 5 minutes, until just barely turning brown at the edges. Serve immediately with vanilla ice cream.

Coconut Crème Brûlée—A Hula Grill Tradition

Crème brûlée is definitely a crowd favorite. We make ours special by flavoring it with coconut. Of course, the fun part of eating crème brûlée is cracking the sugar crust. In the restaurant we use a kitchen torch to melt the sugar topping, but a home broiler works just fine.

SERVES 6 TO 8

INGREDIENTS

3 cups heavy cream
½ cup granulated sugar
10 egg yolks
1½ teaspoons coconut extract
¾ teaspoon vanilla extract
6-12 teaspoons granulated sugar, for topping

PREPARATION

Preheat the oven to 300 degrees F.

Place cream in a saucepan and bring just to a boil over medium heat, stirring frequently to prevent cream from sticking to the bottom of the pan. In a bowl, whisk together sugar and egg yolks. Pour one-third of the hot cream into the egg mixture and whisk to combine, then slowly pour egg mixture into the remaining heavy cream, whisking constantly. (If you add all the hot cream to the egg mixture at once, the eggs will scramble, but adding a small amount of the cream first, warms the eggs more gradually and prevents scrambling.) Add coconut and vanilla extracts, and mix.

Pour custard into ramekins or ovenproof bowls. Place ramekins into a roasting pan and add ¼ inch water to the pan. Place pan in the oven and bake for 45 minutes; remove and chill in the refrigerator for at least 2 hours.

SUGAR CRUST: TORCH METHOD

Remove custards from the refrigerator. Sprinkle the tops of each with 1 to 2 teaspoons sugar to cover evenly. Using a kitchen torch, heat sugar until caramelized. Refrigerate, uncovered, until a hard crust forms.

SUGAR CRUST: BROILER METHOD

Remove custards from the refrigerator. Sprinkle the tops of each with 1 to 2 teaspoons sugar to cover evenly. Preheat the broiler to high. Place chilled ramekins in a roasting pan, add ½ inch ice water to the pan (the water keeps the cream from cooking) and place under the broiler for 5 to 8 minutes, watching closely, until sugar is caramelized. Refrigerate, uncovered, until a hard crust forms.

Passionate Liliko'i Mousse

Liliko'i is what we call passion fruit in Hawai'i; I first tasted it at backyard luaus in the early 1980s. The fruit is often like a sunny-yellow, hard-shelled lemon and grows wild in the mountains on the Big Island. The sweet, gooey, golden insides are used to flavor everything from cake frosting to pudding. I started playing with this simple mousse recipe at The Gallery restaurant in 1986, and people liked it so much that my wife and I served it at our wedding instead of cake. It's been on the menu at Merriman's since day one. A dollop of sweetened whipped cream makes a nice garnish.

SERVES 4

INGREDIENTS
½ cup liliko'i puree or concentrate (often frozen)
4 tablespoons unsalted butter, softened
2 eggs
¼ cup heavy whipping cream

FOR THIS RECIPE, YOU CAN USE:
½ cup liliko'i sweetened frozen puree
    (or concentrate) OR
3 ounces liliko'i puree and 3 ounces sugar
    (mixed together)

At Merriman's, we use liliko'i puree.

PREPARATION
If using frozen liliko'i, thaw and bring to room temperature. Using an electric mixer on low speed, beat liliko'i, butter and eggs together over medium heat in a double boiler for about 3 to 5 minutes, until just before the mixture reaches the very soft peak stage. Let mixture cool. Cover and chill in the refrigerator for several hours. The mixture can be prepared up to a day ahead.

Whip cream into stiff peaks. Gently fold whipped cream into chilled liliko'i mixture until well blended.

ASSEMBLE
Spoon mousse into serving bowls, or get fancy and pipe mousse into the bowls in spiral peaks.

Monkeypod Kitchen by Merriman, Ko'Olina, O'ahu

Chocolate Mochi Cake

This chocolate cake, a Bev Kypfer creation for Merriman's Waimea, is my mother's favorite. You'll notice that the use of rice flour makes this a gluten-free dessert. What you may not realize is that mochiko is a special kind of flour produced from ground cooked rice. In Japan it is used to make the chewy, sweet confection called mochi. It gives this cake a very moist and springy texture. I suggest serving it with whipped cream or a scoop of your favorite ice cream.

SERVES 9 TO 12

MOCHI CAKE

4 tablespoons unsalted butter

6 ounces dark chocolate (70%–85% cacao),
*   broken into small pieces*

2 cups mochiko flour

1½ cups granulated sugar

3 tablespoons cocoa powder

1 tablespoon baking soda

1 teaspoon salt

1½ cups canned coconut milk

1½ cups evaporated milk

1 teaspoon vanilla extract

4 large eggs

PREPARE CAKE

Preheat the oven to 300 degrees F.

Line the bottom of a 13 x 9-inch baking pan with parchment paper.

Melt butter and chocolate in a saucepan over medium-low heat, stirring to mix. When melted, remove from the heat and let cool to room temperature. Measure flour, sugar, cocoa powder, baking soda and salt into a large bowl and whisk to combine completely.

Measure coconut milk into a bowl and shake or lightly whisk to re-combine the separated cream and liquid. Add evaporated milk, vanilla and eggs and whisk to combine. Add liquids to melted butter and chocolate, and mix well. Pour mixture into dry ingredients and whisk until smooth and fully incorporated.

Pour batter into the pan and jiggle gently to remove bubbles. Bake 40 to 50 minutes, until a cake tester or wooden toothpick comes out clean.

Not-Your-Mother's Coconut Layer Cake

This super-rich, sky-high coconut cake is covered with a cloud of classic, pure-white boiled icing and a coating of toasted coconut. It makes a beautiful presentation for a birthday or any special occasion. For the filling between the layers, don't be afraid to get creative. We use some of the boiled icing between the layers, but I also like raspberry jam thinned with Chambord (this recipe), or crushed pineapple works well, as long as it's well drained. The recipe calls for ground coconut, which you can make by processing unsweetened flaked coconut continuously in a food processor for about 1 minute, or until it is as fine as it will get.

MAKES 1 (3-LAYER, 9-INCH) CAKE

CAKE

3½ cups cake flour
2½ cups granulated sugar
1½ tablespoons baking powder
¾ teaspoon salt
1 cup ground unsweetened coconut
12 tablespoons (1½ sticks) unsalted butter,
    very soft but not melted, plus extra for greasing
1½ cups milk
4 egg yolks (save whites for icing)
2 whole eggs
1 cup canned coconut milk, well shaken, or mix the
    separated cream and milk before measuring
1½ tablespoons vanilla extract

PREPARE CAKE

Preheat the oven to 325 degrees F.

Line 3 (9-inch) cake pans with parchment and grease the parchment and sides of the pan with butter.

Sift together cake flour, sugar, baking powder, salt and ground coconut. Place dry ingredients in the bowl of standing mixer. Add butter and mix until no large pieces of butter remain. Add milk and mix on high speed for 1 minute. Scrape down the sides of the bowl. With the mixer running, add egg yolks one at a time, then add whole eggs one at a time. Add coconut milk and vanilla, mixing just until well incorporated, while continuously scraping the bottom and sides of the bowl.

Divide batter evenly among the 3 pans and bake for 30 to 35 minutes, switching the positions of the pans in the oven about halfway through to ensure even baking. Cakes are done when slightly browned on top and a wooden toothpick or cake tester inserted in the center comes out clean.

Cool the pans on wire racks for 10 minutes. Remove cakes from the pans and let cool completely on wire racks.

Recipe continued on page 240

Recipe continued from page 238

FILLING

1 cup raspberry jam

2 tablespoons Chambord
*   or other raspberry liqueur*

PREPARE FILLING

Place jam in a small bowl. Add liqueur, 1 table-spoon at a time, mixing well after each addition.

ICING AND ASSEMBLY

1½ cups unsweetened, flaked coconut

1 cup granulated sugar

⅜ cup light corn syrup

4 tablespoons water

4 egg whites

½ teaspoon vanilla extract

PREPARE ICING

Place sugar, corn syrup and water in a saucepan over medium-high heat. Stir to combine, and cook, without stirring, until syrup comes to a boil. Continue boiling until syrup reaches 235 degrees F (use a candy or instant-read thermometer to check the temperature).

When syrup is almost done, whip egg whites using an electric mixer on high speed, until stiff peaks form. Reserve in the mixing bowl. When syrup is ready, mix egg whites at medium speed while adding hot syrup in a thin stream. Continue until all syrup is added and icing is glossy. Add vanilla and whip at high speed for a few seconds, until incorporated.

ASSEMBLE

Place unsweetened coconut into a skillet and turn heat to medium. Toast, stirring almost constantly, until golden brown, 3 to 5 minutes. Place one cake layer on a plate and spread with half the raspberry jam mixture, then top with a thin layer of icing. Cover with the second cake layer and spread with the remaining filling. Place the final cake layer on top and frost the sides and top generously with the boiled icing. Gently sprinkle and pat toasted coconut onto the top and sides of the cake.

This cake is best when served the same day it is made, so be sure to tell your guests to save room for dessert!

Monkeypod Kitchen by Merriman, Ko'Olina, O'ahu

Bev Kypfer, Pastry Chef

FOR THOSE OF YOU who have always wanted to know the origin of Merriman's Signature Chocolate Purse (page 232), let me introduce Bev Kypfer. Bev and I apprenticed together at the Woodstock Inn from 1979 to 1980, and I do not exaggerate when I say that she was the star apprentice. Bev packs an astonishing amount of talent, an incredible work ethic, and basically no ego into her five-foot frame. (When she cooked on the line, she kept a glassware rack on the floor nearby so she could kick it underneath her feet when she had to reach the shelf over the range.)

After graduation, Bev focused on pastry, honing her skills in restaurant kitchens across the country. In 1992, I finally convinced her to join the Merriman's family as the pastry chef in Waimea, a position she held with skill and grace for 22 years before retiring. There aren't many pictures of Bev; she's shy. And she's not long on conversation, especially when she's working. But her huge influence comes through in her creations.

Bev's pastry style mirrors all Merriman's food—clean, bold flavors that showcase local ingredients. She kept her baking area and tools immaculate, never allowing the baking pans to mingle with other kitchen tools. "Too much chance of grease contamination," she'd say, "That's how you get that icky 'bakery' flavor." Bev has washed all her own pans over her entire career. She personally wiped down every dessert menu every day and stacked them neatly for the waitstaff.

With an irony worthy of O. Henry, Bev the pastry chef has diabetes. She took to distance running, from 5Ks to marathons, to help manage the disease, and she's still racing. Now that she's retired, Bev and her husband, Jay, have more time for adventure travel—like riding the trains of India, and hiking the coast of Scotland. Lucky for us, she left most of her recipes behind.

Richard Ha—Banana King

WHEN THE PHONE RANG on Christmas Day in 1985, I expected the familiar voice of a family member or close friend. Instead, it was a total stranger. "You don't know me," said the caller, "I'm Richard Ha and I have a farm south of Hilo. I've heard about how you're sourcing locally grown produce for your restaurants and are willing to pay a good price. I just want you to know how important this is for the

small farmers." That call meant a lot to me. The Gallery restaurant was still new and I was just barely getting enough of the fresh vegetables I needed. The fact that this stranger from the other side of the island had heard about it meant the word was spreading, and it reassured me that maybe I wasn't crazy to think we could eventually go completely local.

Richard grew up on a farm, but had taken a detour into military service in Vietnam, and then to the University of Hawai'i at Manoa for a degree in accounting. After graduation, he went home to run the family chicken farm. In the mid-1970s he was looking for a crop

to grow on some unused family land, and on a chance trip to the supermarket he saw bananas imported from Central America. *This is insane,* he thought, *why are they importing something we can grow right here in Hawai'i?* So he started trading fertilizer made from chicken waste for baby banana plants. Soon he had the biggest banana farm in Hawai'i.

Over the years, the farm has moved several times—to Kapuu, Keaau and finally to Pepeekeo. "Keaau was a wonderful site, but we always grow the bananas in a couple of locations because of the risk of disease," he told me. And sure enough, a virus struck in Keaau. "We destroyed all of the plants there and moved on because we didn't want it to spread to any neighboring farms."

Richard said that the 2008 spike in oil prices presented another challenge. Farm workers were asking for loans to buy gas to drive to work. "I could see we needed a new business model," he said. He decided to downsize his growing operation in order to rely on the local work force alone. Then he leased the land at the further reaches of the property to his neighbors. That meant the land stayed in production, no one had to drive too far, and local families could make money selling their crops through the new cooperative, Hamakua Springs Country Farms. He calls this a "family of farms" model.

Since then, Richard has devoted much of his time to developing renewable energy sources. The farm generates nearly all of its own electricity via a hydroelectric generator that uses a flume on the property. "I just borrow the water from the stream, run it through the flume, and then put it back," he said with a chuckle. It's just one way he lowers the cost of production so he can keep quality up, while keeping prices reasonable.

Richard is my kind of farmer—growing a superior crop while also looking out for the land and the people of Hawai'i.

Pepeekeo Bananas Foster

Caramel, bananas, and vanilla ice cream—what's not to like? Our twist on this perennial favorite includes lime zest and some coconut cream, plus my friend Richard Ha's locally grown bananas. *Note:* Unsweetened canned coconut cream is not always easy to find, but you can use the top layer of cream that forms in canned, unsweetened coconut milk.

Monkeypod Kitchen by Merriman,
Ko'Olina, O'ahu

SERVES 6

INGREDIENTS

6 tablespoons unsalted butter
¾ cup brown sugar
6 bananas, peeled and cut in half lengthwise and crosswise
1 cup dark rum
Zest of 1 lime
½ cup unsweetened coconut cream
6 scoops vanilla ice cream

PREPARE BANANAS

Heat a sauté pan over high heat, add butter, and cook until the butter is brown and most of the foam has subsided. Reduce heat to medium-high and add sugar, stirring constantly to avoid burning. Cook until sugar dissolves, less than 1 minute. Add bananas and cook for 1 minute on each side. Transfer 4 pieces of banana into each of 6 individual serving bowls.

PREPARE FLAMBÉ SAUCE

Carefully add rum to hot butter-sugar mixture, stirring continuously. If the sugar is very hot, the rum might flame up on its own. Otherwise, flambé using a wand lighter. If sugar crystals form, they will mostly dissolve as you continue to stir the sauce. When the flames subside, stir in lime zest and coconut cream.

ASSEMBLE

Add a scoop of ice cream to the bananas in each bowl. Spoon sauce over bananas and ice cream.

Haupia with Raspberry Sauce

Haupia is a traditional Hawaiian dessert, and if you've ever been to a luau, you might have tasted this jellied, creamy coconut confection. I prefer a softer haupia, more like a dense pudding, and I serve it scooped into a bowl and drizzled with a simple raspberry sauce. *Note:* If you can't find unsweetened coconut cream, you can use the thick cream from the top of canned, unsweetened coconut milk, but you will need about 8 cans of the milk to get enough of the cream.

SERVES 8

INGREDIENTS

2 (14–16-ounce) cans unsweetened coconut cream
4 tablespoons granulated sugar
1/4 teaspoon salt
1/4 teaspoon vanilla extract
5 tablespoons cornstarch
5 tablespoons water
2 tablespoons shredded, sweetened coconut
2 tablespoons unsalted butter

RASPBERRY SAUCE

1/2 cup raspberry jam
3 tablespoons Chambord
    or other raspberry liqueur

PREPARE HAUPIA

Place coconut cream, sugar, salt and vanilla extract into a saucepan. Bring just to a simmer over low heat, stirring constantly. Mix cornstarch with water and stir into the simmering liquid. Stir in shredded coconut. Simmer until mixture thickens, about 20 minutes, stirring frequently. Turn off heat and stir in butter. Pour mixture into a 9 x 11-inch baking pan and chill in the refrigerator for 2 hours.

PREPARE SAUCE

In a small saucepan, mix together jam and liqueur. Stir over low heat just until jam is dissolved.

ASSEMBLE

To serve, spoon haupia into bowls and drizzle with raspberry sauce.

Monkeypod Kitchen by Merriman, Wailea, Maui

Pineapple Upside-Down Cake in a Skillet

Hawaiian pineapples are famously sweet and, when combined with some buttery, brown-sugar caramel and a rich yellow cake, make for a classic dessert. At Merriman's, we make individual cakes, but at home, I prefer using an old-fashioned cast iron skillet and rings of pineapple. If you like, serve it with a small scoop of vanilla ice cream.

MAKES 1 (10-INCH) CAKE

CAKE

12 tablespoons (1½ sticks)
    unsalted butter, divided
¾ cup light brown sugar
½ fresh pineapple, peeled, cored
    and cut into slices ⅜-inches thick
1½ cups flour
1 tablespoon baking powder
3 eggs
½ cup whole milk
1 tablespoon vanilla extract
2 teaspoons almond extract or coconut extract
¾ cup granulated sugar

PREPARE CAKE

Preheat the oven to 350 degrees F.

Heat a 10-inch cast iron skillet over medium-high heat. Add 4 tablespoons of the butter and brown sugar. Stir and cook 1 minute, until sugar is melted. Place pineapple slices side-by-side into the pan and remove the skillet from the heat.

Sift flour and baking powder together into a bowl. In a separate bowl, whisk together eggs, milk, vanilla and almond extract until combined. Using an electric mixer, cream the remaining 8 tablespoons butter with the granulated sugar. In alternating batches, add flour mixture and egg mixture, one-third at a time, to the butter-sugar mixture. Mix well after each addition until smooth, while being careful not to overmix.

Pour cake batter over the pineapple, smoothing the top. Place the skillet in the oven and bake for 40 minutes, or until a toothpick comes out clean. Allow cake to cool for 15 minutes; run a knife between the edge of the cake and the skillet to loosen. Place a large deep plate upside down over the skillet and, wearing oven mitts, carefully invert cake onto the plate. If any pineapple slices stick to the skillet, gently scrape them off and place on the cake. Allow cake to cool completely before slicing and serving.

Monkeypod Kitchen by Merriman, Wailea, Maui

Strawberry Cream Pie à la Monkeypod Kitchen by Merriman

It was Calvin Escorpeso, our longtime dishwasher in Waimea, who reminded me how much we all love cream pies when he showed up one day with his mother's mango cream pie. More than 20 years later, I was working out the dessert menu for our new Monkeypod Kitchen by Merriman. I wanted something pretty and irresistible—the kind of dessert no one can say no to—cream pies! And that's all we offer for dessert at Monkeypod. If you love this pie, you can thank Mrs. Escorpeso.

PIE FILLING

24 ounces cream cheese, softened to room temperature
2¼ cups powdered sugar, divided
2¾ cups heavy cream
1½ tablespoons vanilla extract

PREPARE FILLING

Place cream cheese in a large bowl. Using an electric mixer, whip cream cheese for about 30 seconds. Scrape down sides, add ½ cup of the powdered sugar and continue whipping another 30 seconds to incorporate. Scrape sides again, add ¾ cup of the sugar and continue whipping for 1 minute.

In a clean bowl, place cream, remaining powdered sugar and vanilla. Using an electric mixer, whip into stiff peaks.

Fold 2 large spoonfuls of the whipped cream into the cream cheese mixture, then fold the remaining whipped cream into the mixture, being careful not to overmix. (You should still be able to see some separate waves of cream and cheese.)

Gently spoon filling into the crust, piling it high into a dome. (Depending on the depth of the pan, you may not use all the filling, but pile it as high as you can.) Place pie in the freezer for 2 hours.

STRAWBERRY TOPPING AND SAUCE

1 quart (16 ounces) fresh strawberries, stemmed
3 tablespoons powdered sugar
3 tablespoons guava jelly
1 tablespoon water

PREPARE SAUCE

Slice each strawberry lengthwise into 4 to 5 pieces, reserving the largest flat, leaf-shaped slices. Place the smaller half-round outer slices into a blender or food processor. Add powdered sugar and puree until smooth. Strain out the seeds, using a fine-mesh strainer or 2 layers of cheesecloth, and store resulting sauce in the refrigerator.

ASSEMBLE

Starting at the center, with the strawberries pointing inward, arrange the reserved slices atop the chilled pie, overlapping them upward (like shingles on a roof) to the edge of the pie.

Mix guava jelly with water by heating slightly in a saucepan, or in the microwave, to just barely melt jelly. Spoon melted jelly over the strawberries, starting at the center of the pie and using the back of the spoon to smooth the jelly and form an even glaze.

To serve, drizzle strawberry sauce onto each plate, and place a slice of pie atop the sauce.

MAKES 1 (9-INCH) PIE

PIE CRUST

1 fully baked, ready-made 9-inch crust,
or prepare 1 (9-inch) crust
using your favorite recipe

My Heroes have always been farmers.

- Peter Merriman -

Acknowledgments

Thanks to my mom, Woody, for giving me the inspiration to become a cook, and for being my toughest critic.

To Vicki and our kids, Cody, Ivy and Jessie, who put up with my never-ending food fixation.

To Barbara Pratt, Melanie's sister, for testing and correcting so many recipes.

To Rick Bayless, a great chef and great friend, for writing the Foreword.

To Dennis Hayes, who got us started down the path that led us to this book.

To all the farmers and ranchers who allowed us to invade their beautiful land with cameras.

To Bill Terry, my business partner and fellow kolohe.

To all the Merriman's and Monkeypod team members for countless hours of help, and especially to the chefs at each restaurant.

Index

Italicized page numbers indicate photos.

NOTES